Emily S. Elliot

**I must keep the chimes going, a story of real life**

Emily S. Elliot

**I must keep the chimes going, a story of real life**

ISBN/EAN: 9783337733070

Printed in Europe, USA, Canada, Australia, Japan

Cover: Foto ©ninafisch / pixelio.de

More available books at **www.hansebooks.com**

# I MUST KEEP THE CHIMES GOING.

## A Story of Real Life.

BY

THE AUTHOR OF "COPSLEY ANNALS," &c., &c.

"Church-bells above the starres hearde."—GEORGE HERBERT.

E. P. DUTTON AND COMPANY.

BOSTON: 135, WASHINGTON STREET.
NEW YORK: 762, BROADWAY.
1869.

No Preface is required for the following chapters beyond the statement that the story contained in them is substantially true.

# CONTENTS.

| CHAPTER | | PAGE |
|---|---|---|
| I. | The Message | 9 |
| II. | Christmas at the Brookes' Cottage | 26 |
| III. | First Class and Third Class | 49 |
| IV. | No. 19, Mill Street, Southwark | 75 |
| V. | Martha and the Top Attic Make Friends | 93 |
| VI. | Martha Finds the Coals Heavier | 116 |
| VII. | Martha has Visitors | 137 |
| VIII. | Last Words | 144 |

# I MUST KEEP THE CHIMES GOING.

## CHAPTER I.

### THE MESSAGE.

T was the Sunday before Christmas-day; and the girls of the Rectory Bible Class were coming down the Winthrop Avenue in parties of two and three, after having been dismissed by Mrs. Estridge, the Rector's wife, at the conclusion of her customary afternoon instructions. It was a class composed of the usual materials. There were the girls who were always punctual, and the girl that was always late. There was the dressy girl, whose Sunday array was a source of perpetual astonishment to her com-

panions, and still more to her teacher; and there was the untidy girl, whose garments seemed to be continually on terms of misunderstanding with their wearer and with each other. There was the girl who always seemed to be on the brink of making a successful answer, and who ever stopped short of that result; and the girl who never thought of answering at all. There was the girl who kept on hand a stock of replies fitting any question, and another whose mental machinery worked so slowly as to lead lookers-on to believe it at a standstill; but who, after a time, would produce from depths of thought an answer so satisfactory as to make the same people wonder whether she had not arrived at it by mistake.

And it was the last of these who wished to keep the chimes going, in accordance with the title of the book you are now engaged in reading.

It was the Sunday before Christmas, and a Christmas whereof the cold and frost had a sting in it, somewhat like the small sharp stone by treacherous and unprincipled boys concealed in snowballs, which rouses the fighting element in the assailed. I sometimes wish that many who sigh for "nice old-fashioned Christmases," such as very strong people call those of keenest frost and snow, might try the experiment of spending theirs at Winthrop, situated near the East coast, and about a quarter of a mile from the fens. West-country people know but little of the matter. The South and West winds seem to go for change of air on their own account to that side of the island for the winter months; and the Gulf stream warms it by hot water, to which accommodation there is the satisfactory addition that no water-rate collector will claim payment for the same; and rich children open the Supplement of the "Illustrated London News" on the Saturday before Christmas, and poor children look at its out-spread pictures in the shop windows, and wish themselves the boy with the red comforter who is bringing home holly in his cart, or the girls muffled up in family shawls, on their way to sing carols at the

Squire's, little remembering that to the poor and the old and the sickly the Christmas message, if borne on the keen breath of the East wind, is often followed by another message from regions colder and icier still.

I remember a delightful passage in the Geography book from which we learnt in our youth, wherein, amid statements of latitude and longitude, and names of chief towns, together with the amount of their exports and imports, the author had in a moment of weakness allowed himself to run into two or three lines of familiar description. And in these we were told how the Norway and Lapland women skate along frozen rivers to market, and how at those very markets, all fluids being congealed by means of the cold, milk is sold in blocks and by the pound. I remember wondering that the great Mr. Pinnock, all of whose learning seemed to break out in catechisms for other people, instead of his being satisfied with keeping it to himself, and who as a matter of duty excluded from those catechismal books with grave and gray covers everything that bordered on the enlivening, or that might lead us to imagine towns and places as anything but dots on the map, should have given us such interesting information; and I felt it scarcely honorable when Saturday — in school-rooms commonly called repetition-day — came round, to allow the bit about Lapland to count in my lessons as of the same value as exports and imports. Of course I wished I could skate to market, and invite my brothers to share a slice of milk; and believed that it was only because those in authority over us were old and had no enterprise in their dispositions that they met my desires with the assurance that I should be very thankful to be back again where I was.

"But then," as we agreed afterwards, "we're always assured that we should be better off as we are than in being anything else, and should be told the same even if we wished for gold watches, or to live in Swiss cottages on mountains, and hunt chamois, or to go and discover new worlds like Columbus, or anything different from lessons." So we rejected our counsel, and wished still for Lapland, and milk by the pound.

Which brings me back to my statement — an echo of the once discarded testimony of our more experienced elders — that West-country people, wishing for a real sharp old-fashioned Christmas, may travel to it by taking a ticket for Winthrop, in East Norfolk, and will in like manner find their first position the best. At least, they might so have done in the winter of which I am writing, and in which Mrs. Estridge's girls were coming down the Rectory Avenue as already mentioned.

I have said that they were girls very much of the usual description; and their conversation, as they grouped and regrouped themselves, was for the most part such as any dozen of country maidens, after an hour's intercourse with one of the two ladies of the village, might be expected to hold. Who had said her verses without a mistake; and who had broken down in the duty to her neighbor; and the dress Mrs. Estridge had worn; and how she had asked Jane Morris for her sailor brother; and how fortunate Susan had been in sitting next the fire; and how careful the Rector's lady had been to see that Mary Harris was wrapped up, and had hoped her cold wouldn't be worse for coming out;—these, and such topics, were quite enough for the talkers, whilst some true children of the Norfolk soil contented themselves with walking on side by side with little or no remark.

"You'll be gone next Sunday, Martha," said one of the talkers to a short, square, quiet-looking girl who had been specially noticed by Mrs. Estridge as having attended her class for the last time. "I wish I was going too. It'd be summut of a change. You'll be coming back a lady; or least ways, with a bonnet like Miss Graham's in church this morning, more like a crown in a picture-book than aught else."

"No, I won't," was the sturdy reply. "I wouldn't be stared at for finery—not if I had a chance."

"I wonder if you'll meet with that Miss—I forget her name—that sent the message to us all. How faithful Mrs. Estridge gave it out."

"I'd know her again," was Martha's reply; "and from the ways of her, she wouldn't take it amiss if I was to cross the road and speak to her. I will if she comes to London."

This was a good deal for Martha to say; and while it implied some ignorance of the likelihood that two strangers, though in London at the same time, might fail to meet each other directly, it betrayed that deep down in her mind the message to which her companion alluded had been put away never to be lost.

Nearly a year before the opening of our story, a friend of Mrs. Estridge's, spending a Sunday at Winthrop, had consented to share with her the Sunday afternoon teaching; and the words that she had spoken had often by the Rector's wife been recalled to the minds of the girls, while in their purport they had from week to week been repeated. And on this particular afternoon Mrs. Estridge had, before parting, read to them a few lines from a letter received only the day before, of which the words were as follows: —

"And tell your girls from me that I send them all good Christmas wishes; and that they must always keep the true Christmas chime ringing in their hearts — 'THANKS BE UNTO GOD FOR HIS UNSPEAKABLE GIFT.'"

Not very much had been added to the message thus repeated — only a few words of what the Gift was, which is truly the unspeakable gift of Christmas-tide — words few enough to be soon forgotten by the careless, and enough to be carried away with the message by the thoughtful, while Mrs. Estridge had bidden them think, when the chimes should ring in Christmas-day, that the church-bells must ring in their heart-temples too.

Martha Brooke's home was on the very edge of the fens, and to it she now returned. A great change in her life was to come in the course of the week now opening. On the day after Christmas-day she was to go to service in London; and to this change she had long looked forward, not with any particular expectation of satisfaction, but simply as that which would come to her in her turn as it had come to her sisters before her.

When Eliza — the first to start forth into the unknown whirl of London life — had gone, her younger sisters had felt as much eagerness of curiosity as in their quiet way it was possible for them to show. They wondered how she must feel at the idea of a railway journey in the new dress and strong boots which were the results of so many savings, and half wished their time for going out had arrived. But Jane had followed since then; and Martha began to feel it such a matter of course that she should go, now that Kezia was old enough to take her place at home, that she did not allow herself to think of her own departure as a matter of much moment to any one but herself.

For Martha was not a girl who looked forward very carefully from one day to another. She accepted her life as she found it, and supposed that it was all right, or at least that what was wrong in it couldn't be helped. It was not pleasant to be always scolded by her mother; but then other girls were scolded too. Her father was a quiet man who seldom spoke, and still more seldom gave any sign of her belonging to him. She had read of fathers who loved, and even showed forth love to, their children, and whose hearts were towards them; but then, as she came to reflect upon it, that was generally in Joseph and his brethren and the Prodigal Son, and in books which must have taken it from them; and as many fathers round her beat and abused their children, she said to herself that, on the whole, she was well off.

And such a conclusion implied a very great amount of thought on Martha's part. She had never known anything very pleasant in her life until the day from which everything that had since been at all pleasant dated. Her home was, on the whole, more respectable than many by which it was surrounded. No particular wrong or shame had cast a shadow over it, although, had such been the case, neither father nor mother would have very keenly felt such a shadow. Every one in the house had been on a working level. The children had been sent to school with a general impression that it would go into work afterwards; and to church, with an idea, equally vague on Mrs. Brooke's part, that so much religion having been got through in the time of childhood, it would be set to her and their account in some shape hereafter. She herself had seldom been to church since she married. When there was a death in the family, she put a black ribbon across her bonnet and appeared in the aisle; and after Christmas gifts from the Parsonage, she "went to church for the blankets," as she expressed it, regarding it as a suitable return compliment to the clergyman; but beyond this, and the registering of each new birth in a Family Bible, which action was regarded by both her and her husband as a religious rite, Mrs. Brooke's Christianity did not go. And though it is pleasant to read of Christian England, and of village piety, and of rural virtue, if the truth were written, of how many village homes is this only too favorable a specimen!

Martha's first gleam of real individual sunshine had, figuratively speaking, crossed her path on the day that Mrs. Estridge, newly arrived at Winthrop, had called and invited her to come up to the Rectory on the Sunday afternoon. Martha could not at first realize, as she stood at the wash-tub with hands deep in soap-suds, that her appearance would make any difference to the lady; but Mrs. Estridge, all the same, looked kind and pleasant about it; and Mrs. Brooke, after having first said she didn't see what the girl was to get by going, was brought round to believe that she wouldn't get any harm, and it wouldn't take out of working time; and finally agreed to allow it.

That was three years ago, and Martha had seldom absented herself since. And underneath the hard outer life there came to be very deep down, and almost unconsciously to herself, a swelling of heart, and a putting forth of feelers and yearnings for a better and higher life; and then had followed strange desires and hopes, and unspoken, unacknowledged notions that all that was said in church, and had been read out at school when she was a child, might have something real in it, something true, and living, and present — something for her. It was as yet only a sort of twilight speculation on Martha's part, and one at first so strange, that she had to take earnest counsel with herself before she could believe that such was the case. The seeds planted in her heart had their place so deep down, that all their first life-strength seemed to be put forth underground, and to expend itself in roots and unseen fibres; and although, because she had not yet grasped visibly to herself those wonderful things to which her life was tending, she believed herself to be very far from them, she was in truth being numbered amongst those who hunger and thirst after righteousness, and who shall be filled.

It was a cold East wind that blew up across the fens as she descended the slope to her own home on the Sunday afternoon, of which

I have spoken :—a cold, sarcastic wind, which however bravely you might fight it at one corner, met you with a keen retort round the next, and made people who thought about it at all wonder where it was originally compounded, and from what recipe for a freezing-mixture it was made up. And Martha, as she stamped sturdily down the frozen road, and drew her shawl closely round her, wondered whether it would meet her like that in London; and then, musing on her London life to come, went over the words which had been in her heart ever since she left the Rectory.

"I must keep the chimes going," that was what the message said ;—Thanks be unto God for His unspeakable gift. The Christmas chimes! I seem to understand it somewhere about me, and not to get hold of it right side foremost. It'll come right best if I think of the unspeakable gift first. The Bible tells us "the gift of God is eternal life through Jesus Christ our Lord." It's that eternal life that's the Christmas gift, because Jesus Christ was born then to die instead of me—to take all my punishment for me, that there might be nothing between me and heaven. It seems almost too much to think, that when He has so much to do, and all the angels to look after, and everyone in great London and towns to mind, that He should care to put the gift right down to me for me to take it up. But then the Bible says so. I wouldn't tell a lie, I know, and He wouldn't, much more. So there it is promised: and I may have it, and I've asked, and I will get it from Him—" eternal life through Jesus Christ our Lord." What a good thing it would be to have that for my Christmas present this year! And why shouldn't I make quite sure? I'd take that away with me into London, and never lose it.

If only I could understand about the chimes! They'll ring out on Christmas-day, and perhaps I'll get hold of the meaning then. If I can't, I'll go up and ask Mrs. Estridge to make it plainer, because I'm so slow. Anyhow, there's something wonderful in believing all about Christmas being something for now, as well as an old story about Christ's coming.

It's wonderful that I once never knew how to ask Jesus to come into my heart where there's room for Him to live always. I sometimes can't believe I'm only plain Martha Brooke, that's got to Him in my slow, clumsy sort of fashion for the unspeakable gift, and hope to be getting it all the same as if I was the Squire's lady herself. For it's promised sure and fast, and He bought it for us;—only I must try and make it out quite plain—that about keeping the Christmas chime in my heart for always.

## CHAPTER II.

### CHRISTMAS AT THE BROOKES' COTTAGE.

THE chimes rang out of Winthrop church-towers on Christmas-day, and the congregation came in; the crisp snow on the churchyard paths sparkling and gleaming in the cold sunshine. All the regular attendants were there, and a sprinkling of irregular ones, who came to see the evergreens round the pillars and arches, and to hear the singing, and with a general notion that church-going in the morning was the right sort of prelude to the Christmas dinner later on.

The family from the great house were early in their pew; the Squire himself looking like an embodiment of Church and State as he walked up the aisle with the important tread customary to him at the Quarter Sessions and on other public occasions. And in Mrs. Graham's face, which was wont to be sharp and thin, there appeared a sort of consciousness that coals and blankets had not been forgotten the day before; while old Mapper, the clerk, ostentatiously preceded her with a bright red comforter round his neck, which he wished her to understand was the same which had accompanied his donation of coals on the previous evening, and which he wore as a mark of respect; his grandsons figuring under the gallery in other comforters, of which the rather washed-out glories proclaimed them as the Christmas gifts of former years. And the young ladies tried to appear as if they had not been the decorators of the chancel, and knew nothing about the wreath over the arch, or the "Glory to God in the highest" round the east window, although it was well understood that they and their brothers had been busy among holly and ivy wreaths the whole of the previous day. Only little Effie, who being but nine years old, was not supposed to be indifferent to her own share in the handiwork, was heard to whisper to Mr. John: "And I held all the white holly for the G in 'Glory,' and Mary wouldn't let me make the letters; but I will next Christmas;" for which remark, although intensely interesting to the girls who sat in the choir on the open bench before the squire's pew, Effie was immediately quenched by an admonitory glance from her elder sister.

Then Mrs. Estridge came in with Harry and Gracie, and took her seat on the opposite side of the chancel; and Effie and Gracie had to be restrained by their respective guardians from holding telegraphic communication concerning the glories of the wreath round the arch. And then Mr. Estridge came out of the vestry, and the Confession and the Prayers were read; and concerning the Child of Bethlehem all voices sang, "Thou art the King of Glory, O Christ!" and all voices said, "I believe in Jesus Christ, our Lord, who sitteth at the right hand of God: from thence He shall come again to judge both the quick and the dead."

I wonder whether many people think of what they are saying in the Creed. In old days the Teutonic nobles used to draw their swords, and repeat the words while their glittering blades flashed in the air, to show that they would be willing to fight and die for the faith — for the faith in Him who came as a child into the world that He might die for us. I sometimes think, that though in England people do not draw swords from their sheaths when they say the Creed, those who love His name and who remember how for them He was crucified, dead, and buried, have something of the fighting spirit roused in their hearts by the old old words, and long to overcome and be set down with Him on the throne of His glory, even as He also overcame and was set down with the Father on His throne.

The winter's sun was shining brightly through the stained glass of the east window when the choir struck up, "Hark, the herald angels sing!" "The unspeakable gift," thought Martha to herself; "no wonder angels brought the message, and then couldn't find any such words for it as 'Glory to God in the highest, and on earth peace, good-will toward men.' I like that 'good-will;' it seems as if we was wanted to have the gift each one." And Martha's voice, which was full and clear, went out with a real joy such as nothing particular in her outward life had ever occurred to call forth, in the song,

> "Joyful all ye nations rise,
> Join the triumph of the skies;
> With the heavenly hosts proclaim,
> Christ is born at Bethlehem."

She wondered at her own happiness as she sang. "And yet I ought to be glad," she said to herself; "He came for me. When one thinks of it, at first it seems more natural that rich people should have the great gifts, like they have everything else, and for us poor plain ones to be passed over. I haven't a grand cloak like the young ladies from the great house, all richness, and, taken in one light, like silk, and in the other like bird's feathers, just where they turn soft and downy; and I'm not pretty, like Mrs. Estridge, but plain and awkward. But the unspeakable gift's for me all the same — it says so: 'unto all people;' like a letter directed to me in my own name; and it seems like something for always in one's heart to remember, 'eternal life through Jesus Christ our Lord.'"

Martha did not know that the joy-bells, the true Christmas-chimes, were already ringing in her heart as she sang out so gladly. She only knew that she was not left out of the day's rejoicing, and that the reason why she was glad was because the Christ born at Bethlehem was her Saviour, and that he was near to her for ever.

Everybody was wishing everybody else happy Christmases after service. Even the squire, who by nature was silent and did not notice people, nodded to the groups in the churchyard, as if he couldn't do less on the 25th of December; and Mrs. Estridge went amongst all her village friends, shaking hands, and asking after rheumatisms and coughs, and saying how cold it was, and how she hoped everybody would enjoy themselves, in a manner which Martha admired from a distance, wondering all the time whether she would herself come in for a greeting, but feeling far too shy even to look as if she lingered in expectation of such distinction.

It came, however — the kind word and touch of the hand upon her shoulder, and pleasant smile, which, far more than Mrs. Estridge could have believed, went to make her Christmas a happy day, sending a little electric thrill of pleasure through the quiet country girl, for which she could hardly account, even to herself.

"Your last day with us, my child! I hope it will be a happy one. But I shall miss you on Sundays. Remember you are to let me know how you get on in London: and, Martha, Christmas can be kept in our hearts all the year round, can't it? We must try to let the true Christmas chime be always ringing, you know."

And then Mrs. Estridge went to join her husband, and there was a sore feeling in the girl's heart as she watched her as far as the Rectory Avenue: and very much to her own surprise, everything round looked quite dim in spite of the bright sunshine that streamed down on the snowy pathways. What was over her? Martha could hardly believe that great tears were welling up into her eyes in an unwonted manner as she recalled the last words of the friend to whom she had slowly and week by week been making the offering of true deep gratitude and affection; and then she tried to remember how it had felt to have Mrs. Estridge's hand laid on her shoulder, and asked herself if it could be possible that she meant what she said about missing her, and thought how she had finished with the words, "We must keep the chime going." "As if we would be together in something," she said to herself; "and I will, oh, I will; I'll try and remember always, always! I would, if it was only for love of her, I would; but it's more than that,— I have the Unspeakable Gift given to me, and I'll never forget it as long as I live!

It was dinner-time when she reached home, and Mrs. Brooke was, with Kezia's help, putting the beef and pudding on the table, which had been in part supplied from the great house the day before.

I wonder whether any but true-born English people can enter into the full meaning and sentiment of Christmas pudding, — the institution which penetrates into the humblest cottages, into workhouses, and even into prisons, in which last retreat it is regarded, as a general rule, with much more respect than the law of the land. Foreigners may make, may eat, and may even go as far as to enjoy the same; but with a rightly-constituted Englishman or Englishwoman, consciously or unconsciously, there belongs to every mouthful a sense of nationality, of hereditary Church and State attachment, together with an infusion of as much family feeling as it is possible to muster, all of which go to form an invisible compound, served up at the same time with the material embodiment of groceries and other ingredients, and giving a flavor and meaning to the same which can be attained on Christmas-day only, and then only by the home-born.

Mrs. Brooke at one time in the year seemed able to look over the deeply-worn groove of her work-a-day life, and to realize, with a momentary approach to the dignity of a British matron, her position as a wife and mother of a family. It was when, with the only approach to sentiment which she was ever known to exhibit, she stuck a sprig of holly, " to give a touch of feeling." as she annually expressed it, in the centre of the pudding. and then sat down at the head of her family to eat it.

Even in the poor cottage on the fens there arose, at the observance of the yearly festival, a remembrance of the absent members of the family. The Brookes were at all times so slow of speech, were so fixed in a sort of belief that what was to be was, which thing, in their case, happened to be, from time to time, the due exportation into London service of one of the children, that, this transaction having been accomplished, little was said about the matter; unless it chanced that Mrs. Brooke, in scolding the daughters that remained, would finish up with, "'Liza now, hur *was* good for summut; hur knew how to stir round, hur did;" which generally resulted in a practical exemplification on her own part of what "stirring round" might be supposed to signify, much to the bewilderment and disturbance of the different members of the household.

Over the pudding, however, the father of the family, who had arrived at an idea that he should, before parting from her, "throw out a word to Patty," as he expressed it to himself, concerning her new start in the world, began to work up to it by slow degrees, to the manifest approbation of his wife, who, coarse and rough-hewn as was her ordinary life, had, at the bottom of it all, a certain womanly satisfaction in any approach on her husband's part to recognitions of his family relationship in partnership with herself.

"'Liza, now, she's a eating of pudding

somewheres, I'll be bound," was the paternal observation which, in an unwonted manner, betrayed his remembrance of the absent.

"It don't seem only like two years since hur was away," continued his wife, carrying on the train of thought. "It was a bigger pudding that year than this. Mrs. Law, she takes a bit off for every one as goes; that's what I've minded each year. There was a handful of raisins less after 'Liza went, and a quarter of a pound less suet after Jane was off. I'm thinkin' we'll lose by Patty's going next year; and if I can, I'll have speech with one of the young ladies up at the house, and ask to know if it's by their desires."

From which remark the reader will discover that Mrs. Law was the Squire's housekeeper; and further, that the charities over which she presided were dispensed not altogether with the inconsiderateness of generosity to which the season of Christmas is supposed to conduce.

"There's Jane, too," continued Mr. Brooke, after a longer silence than the first, during which second slices had been given round; "I shouldn't wonder if *she* was a eatin' of puddin' now at this very minit;" in pursuing which train of thought his wife looked at the clock, and observed that it was pretty nigh gone one, whereupon the children looked at the clock too, and as it struck, seemed in their turn struck with their father's idea.

He himself was rising in spirits in the unusual process of conducting a family conversation, his habit being on most other days in the year to devour hungrily and silently what might be prepared for him in the interval of his labor, indulging now and then only in an angry exclamation against his wife, if his usual allowance was wanting in weeks of scant wages, or of other difficulty.

Christmas-day was telling upon him, however, as in the bosom of his family he gave vent to a third remark, which was founded on the pattern of the former ones, as they had proved successful.

"Patty, now; she'll be eatin' of puddin' somewheres next year, you may depend."

Martha grew very red as she felt that all the eyes round the table were bent upon her, while her mother, with a dim idea that, tomorrow being a working day, it would be time saved to say what was necessary to her daughter at parting then and there, nodded to her husband, and then to Martha, and then to the other children, repeating his words as being what they might all take note of: " Patty, yes, hur'll be eatin' of puddin' somewheres next year;" adding the exhortation, " Now, Martha, you mind that; that's from father and me."

It might have occurred to an unenlightened listener that, regarded as parting advice, the remark relating to Martha's next year's consumption of Christmas pudding, was hardly such as practically to bear with much force upon her future career; but I don't think that any such idea presented itself to her or to any one else at table. On the contrary, there was a certain approach to maternal dignity, and even kindliness, in the words, " that's from father and me." which, while it convinced Mr. Brooke that he had offered a very original and well-timed remark, found its way, though slowly, to Martha's heart; while a sort of yearning came over her towards the rough, coarse, and generally loveless home, from which on the next day she was to drift into an individual life of her own.

"Yes, mother," she answered, rather humbly.

"Ay: it's all in that what your mother says," continued her father, willing in some sort to pay back his wife's appreciation of his former remarks, "hur said 'moind.' Now, Patty, you *moind*. It's what I says to Jane, and to 'Liza before her, when they was goin'. And it won't wear out afore its Kezia's turn. You allers moind, and then, as I says, you'll be moinded of." Whereupon Mrs. Brooke hinted that the parson himself would find it hard to improve upon that, and told Martha "not to forget her bringin' up or her schoolin';" and when Martha had said she wouldn't, added, "and you fulfil that sitiwation that you're summonsed to, and you'll be like the other two, never coming back like a bad penny on our hands."

With which burst of feeling, and the finishing up of the pudding, Martha's exhortation on leaving the parental roof ended; and, indeed, the Christmas observance in the Brookes' house also found its close. The dishes were put away, and Mrs. Brooke was heard to remark to Kezia " out at the back," that she felt most lost after dinner was over whenever Christmas-day came, for that, look at it in one way, it seemed most as dull as Sundays for work; and, look at it the other, why, it seemed a waste not to be settin' to the washin', " which I wouldn't think nothin' before I'd be at it now," she concluded, " if it wasn't for neighbors sayin' as we couldn't afford to sit like gentlefolks for Christmas-day, which, after all, comes but once a year."

Martha, meanwhile, was busy upstairs in packing up her few possessions, much as her sisters had done before her. Her Bible and Prayer-book, given her at school, and her working clothes, and a few other little properties, sufficient to form a bundle, were tied up in an old shawl ready for the morrow's journey. The three younger children looked on with a vague wonder and admiration, while she told them that on the next day she would be going away from them in the train, together with that identical bundle; and then they ran off to play, leaving her to finish up her work by herself, which she did, wondering almost as much as they as to what it would feel like, to be, for the first time, away from them all, and starting life on her own account.

And then, when all was done, and when Mrs. Brooke had sent Kezia out to the farm to get the milk, and had settled herself to sleep in the one arm-chair by the fire, Martha arrayed herself in her new warm shawl, the result of deposits in Mrs. Estridge's clothing club, and put on the brown straw bonnet which she had worn for the first time that morning, and, in the unwonted leisure of Christmas afternoon, took the road leading up to the church. A settled purpose was in her mind,— the accomplishment of a plan which she had formed for this last day at home, after the Bible class of the previous Sunday,—and, in the freezing cold of approaching dusk, she drew her shawl round her closely, and tried to think out with something of distinctness, the feelings which were deep down in her heart, but for which, even to herself, she could not find expression. If she could have known it, they were gentle and tender ones,—gentler and tenderer than might naturally have been nurtured in a hard, religionless home,—feelings which had come to her with the longing for the higher life towards which her heart had been drawn by kindly words and heavenly influences,—longing, upward-tending thoughts, which now were beginning to raise themselves with new, vigorous shoots above the coarse soil of an ignorant and rough every-day life, filling her with a strange sense of purpose, and meaning, and hopefulness, such as she had never, until lately, understood or imagined.

The slope up to Winthrop Church was the prettiest bit of the village; and the churchyard trees were looked upon with some pride by the inhabitants. Through the gate Martha took her way, and down the path to the furthest end of the enclosure; and then she stopped by a grave with a small head-stone, on which the inscription was but of recent date. The words engraved were only

  Mary Lee, *died* 18—. *Aged* 15.

"I'm glad to come here," said Martha to herself, as she stood by the tomb of a young girl who had died some months before, and whom she had cared for as for few other village companions; "I helped to carry her to the grave here, and I'll think of her often when I'm gone away. She wasn't long ill, but she had the Unspeakable Gift. I mind how she said before she died that she wasn't feared to die, because He had died for her, and that He was everything she wanted. I wonder whether there are chimes up in heaven to ring at Christmas-time. I wonder whether Mary's listening to them. I think if I was to go to heaven, I'd like to keep Christmas even more than down here; seeing Him who came to be a child, that He might give His life for ours. But, somehow, it seems a long way off; something so far out of one's way. Work, and being followed round by mother, and washing up, and all, seems realer than all about Him. But then, death's as true as all that. Mary died —" and at this point Martha found herself touching the grave-stone, as if to assure herself that it was there, telling a true tale — "Mary died, and then she found it all as it's written for us, about the golden streets, and harpers with their harps, and the tree of life, and all; and it was having the Unspeakable Gift that took her safe there; the great gift of Jesus Christ. I think I'm rather glad some one I know has gone over there, because of it. It makes me feel more as if it was the only thing that's to last always. Yes. I'm glad Mary's there; and I'll know her when I've got to thank Him for it all. It feels like a sort of showing out that it's all true what we're told of, — dying and heaven, — to have her gone where there's no trouble nor worry, nor being scolded for anything any more."

With which thoughts Martha turned to look round again over the village churchyard, still with the intense stillness of the winter frost and winter twilight. The damps had risen from the marshy grounds below the slope on which she stood, and the firm road through the fens, stretching on out of sight, looked like the old Bible pictures of the pathway of the children of Israel through the cloud and the sea. And high above the mists and vapors, which came up like waves from the lower flats, a clear crescent moon was shining, and sentinel stars were standing out like watchers in the sky; and it seemed to Martha as if the shadows of the trees, with the rime upon their branches, and the deeper shadows of the church, were in some sort thrown over the graves as a night-covering for those sleeping underneath; sleeping as peacefully as little Mary Lee, whom she would never see again.

And just then, as for a last greeting on the Christmas afternoon, the chimes rang out through the stillness. Martha could not tell herself why she liked so much to hear them, or why she was glad that she had been on the the other side of the tower from that by which the bell-ringers entered, so that they seemed to her more like voices from above than the result of efforts within.

"The chimes! they're to remind me once more of the Unspeakable Gift!" she said to herself. "I wonder how it goes. One, two, three, four, five. No, it won't do like that;" and in vain she tried to set the words to the music of Winthrop peal. But suddenly, after a pause, the ringers changed their chime. Slowly the first four bells sounded, and then the full cadence: then again four; then once more the clear octave of notes, ringing, ringing out the reminder, far and near, that the Child of Bethlehem is Christ the Lord.

"That's it," said Martha, joyfully; "I've got it now. I'll be able to keep them in my heart just as the message said:—

"'THANKS BE TO GOD

"'FOR HIS UNSPEAKABLE — GIFT.'

"'*Thanks be to God: For His unspeakable — Gift.*' I'll try and mind about it when I'm tired or put out. I'll try and mind about it down at London that's so big. I'll try and mind about it Sundays and work-a-days, and Christmas days too,—that the great Gift was given for me; and so I've never cause to care for anything that's to worry or vex me, unless it's losing hold of that; and I don't think He'll let me lose hold of it. I'll try and live like it. I want to give my life back to Him who gave Himself for me; and I'll try, O I *will* try to set the bells ringing in my heart; and whatever comes, it won't seem very bad if only I can keep the Christmas chime going."

And then Martha once more looked over to the misty fens, and gave a farewell glance to the mound beneath which Mary Lee was sleeping; and under the shadow of the church found her path among the graves, and wondered, as she went on her way home, that she should have understood so well what Winthrop chimes had to say to her.

## CHAPTER III.

### FIRST CLASS AND THIRD CLASS.

PEOPLE who travel from city to city first class express, gain in time, gain in importance, and probably gain in comfort; but I am inclined to believe that in some respects they have not altogether the advantage over slower travellers. They have opportunities, indeed, of reflection concerning the hurry and bustle of this sublunary life during the brief space of time which may intervene between their settling themselves in corner seats with newspaper, magazine, and sandwiches in store, and the moment of punctual and loudly-signalled departure. They may discover objects not devoid of interest in anxious travellers unable to reconcile themselves to enforced separation from some cherished portmanteau or box of fragile ware, between which and their owners there is this much in common that the last, like their boxes, seem to have "*Care: this side up,*" written visibly on their brows. They may find food for meditation in watching newly-married couples taking possession of coupés, and people barely in time rushing into wrong carriages and being transferred at the last moment to their proper places by watchful officials, and in manifold other transactions, suggestive of stir, and hurry, and change, and busy life. And, if not wholly engrossed in anxieties concerning their own personal well-being, they may discern suggestive themes for thought in the various callings and nationalities represented by the Bishop, and the doctor, and the man of business, and the commercial traveller, and the native servant, and the various other personages collected and jostled together in a confusion which is only brought to an orderly solution by the magic words, "Take your seats."

But to my mind the more leisurely traveller is often the gainer, who, all things being estimated by comparison, saunters through the counties, stopping at village stations, and at way-side gates, and at obscure hamlets, with names so little known, as not even to be counted worthy of publication, being supposed to interest only natives of the soil. The nineteenth century, and gas, and steam, and machinery, and radical reform have not yet erased all English country life. The great red-brick creeper, which branches forth from the large towns, and, in suburban lines of building, calling themselves Prospect Villas and Pleasant Rows, invades quiet meadow tracts, never more to be named as "the country," has not yet overspread the whole of our land. And still, even where the railway echoes are heard as accustomed sounds, English village life is going on, and men and women are living out their histories under the shadow of the church where they were christened, only shaking their heads over the next generation, and saying that "changes have come up since the old days, I believe you."

And little home pictures of country life, whereof the way-side platform with its few accessories of embellishment or comfort is the groundwork, may from time to time be seen by the passing traveller, who, possibly, at many previous stations has heard no disturbance of the stillness beyond the solitary footstep of the guard and the subdued panting of the engine;—pictures sometimes of parting, sometimes of greeting, but all more or less invested with an increase of interest and individuality by reason of the quiet and the loneliness of the framework in which they are set.

Here the nobleman's family is seen to emerge from first-class carriages; and a brief bustle of waiting servants, and loudly-claimed luggage, breaks the monotony of the journey; while lookers-on, who may happen to be well informed concerning the neighborhood, point out to more ignorant fellow-travellers the direction of the country-seat towards which the coronetted carriage is already turning, commonly finishing up with a brief biography of Lord De Blank — "not much good in the county — mostly abroad; but finer timber not to be seen in England, sir; and they do say that the young lord will take to the family place — he that married Sir John Acres' daughter in the next county — a fine place, too, Acres' Park, and Sir John knows something of farming, and goes for a pretty tight landlord. There, you may see the Blankhurst chimneys over behind those trees!" And then the train goes on its way, and other woods and meadows are skirted in its course, and the Blankhurst parenthesis in the afternoon journey is left behind.

And sometimes may be seen a life-parting, and sometimes a greeting of the soldier returned from long absence. And sometimes Mary going to her first place at the country parsonage, is met by a strange fellow-servant, who "supposes she is the young person as is expected," and who, finding that she is, adopts her bonnet-box, while Mary claims the heavy one from the luggage-van. And sometimes the Squire returning from Quarter Sessions, or from a day's sport over the stubble, and sometimes the town young lady friend met with the pony-carriage by her country young lady friend, and "the cart will come down for your boxes, dear," are the foremost figures in the little home histories for a few moments acted out before the eyes of passing travellers. And now and then chimes from a village spire, or the sound of the afternoon organ practice from the church, or the evening hymn swelling through the open windows of a school, or the scents of summer things borne up from cottage gardens, have a message for the passers-by not altogether without power to revive old associations, or to waken up quiet songs without words in secret heart-chambers, if the world's care and work have not done their part in silencing its inner music.

The point at which the narrow stream of Winthrop life joined the tide of world history and nineteenth century civilization was a wayside platform at which only slow trains condescended to stop; and there, some time before the morning parliamentary had become due, Martha Brooke might have been seen, the day after Christmas, escorted by her sister Kezia, and grasping the bundle of which mention has been already made, with a sort of unspoken conviction that all she had now to do was to keep a firm hold on the properties therein contained.

On occasion of the first launch of a daughter into service, two years before, both the father and mother of the Brooke family had come up to Winthrop gate, as they expressed it, "to see the last of 'Liza;" and to the said Eliza there had come a certain dignity and sense of independence, as she kissed the children, and promised to bring them things when she came to see them again. But the family ceremonial had been conducted with less importance when Jane had followed in her sister's track — her father having said that he "saw no good in having to make up after hours along of the girl's going off, which mother could see to better than him." Martha's departure at the Christmas-tide of which we are writing was even less honored in its accompaniments, the thing having to a certain extent become common in the family; so that upon her sister alone devolved the duty of speeding her on her way, Mrs. Brooke having declared, over her wash-tub, that "'twould take a deal to make up all the time wasted in keeping Christmas, special now that they'd be a hand short without Patty, when she was gone."

To the same platform there drove up, just before the arrival of the expected train, the carriage from the great house; and the sisters, looking on, did not take long to come to the conclusion that Miss Graham was also about to start on her travels.

There was what seemed to them an endless quantity of luggage, with the amount of brass and leather displayed in the construction thereof which is generally to be regarded as an outward sign and symbol of the excellence of the contents. And then many charges were given to Green, the lady's maid, as to her care of Miss Dora during her absence. "And you'll be sure to see that she wraps up going

FIRST CLASS AND THIRD CLASS.

P. 56.

out driving," Martha heard Mrs. Graham say, as the train drew up; and then furs and cloaks, and a hot-water footstool, were by the man-servant placed in a corner seat, and the Squire was seen to slip something into the guard's palm as he promised to mind and see after the young lady, who, meantime, looked very bright and merry as she started off for a month of Christmas gaieties, and laughingly told her parents not to mourn for her absence. Then once more Green, who was made to sit opposite to her, was exhorted to take care of her young mistress; and her father, as the whistle sounded, was heard to say, " The carriage will be waiting for you at Shoreditch;" and then, Martha having been deposited in her place, and a brief kiss having sealed the parting of the sisters, the train glided away, and Winthrop tower faded in the distance. and the chapter of her village life was closed and over — not a very happy life — by no means a gentle or tender one — but still life with a home in it, and with a rough sort of family love belonging to it, the remembrance of which brought a swelling into Martha's heart, while she wondered in what sort of a place she would sleep that night.

"Reckon there's a deal of store set by some one over there," was the first remark she heard from a laboring man who pointed backwards with his thumb towards the carriage occupied by Miss Graham and her maid. And Martha, having no reason to think to the contrary, reckoned that there was.

"Comes to the same thing in the end," observed her companion, with some conscious philosophy; adding, after a pause, "First class or third, it's all one at the end — when the journey's over."

Which remark set Martha, who was on her first journey, thinking with much energy, as of late had been her wont.

Has the reader heard of a certain cloth called mungo? Not a superfine or even a showy product of northern looms or steam-mills, but a coarse and strong material which, because it cannot be called fine, styles itself serviceable. It may be that, long before the close of this century, all remembrance of the origin of its name will have passed away; and therefore, reminded of the same by a sympathetic interest in the workings of Martha Brooke's mind, we are willing here to make mention thereof.

Not, as at first might appear probable, is reference in anywise intended to the celebrated African explorer who was indebted to his godfathers and godmothers for a Christian name not commonly to be found in baptismal registers; but to a circumstance attending the production before a Lancashire master manufacturer of coarse shreds of old cloth, carpet, and other woollen textures, with a protest to the effect that they were too rough and valueless to be worked up into a new cloth.

"They wunna go," said the foreman, discouragingly.

"But they *mun go*," replied the master. And hence mungo cloth.

I have sometimes thought that all round us, if only we might take note of the matter, mind-machinery, possibly rough and slow in its operations, is working up out of imperfect notions and common observations, and out-of-the-way ideas, a web of home-spun thought and feeling, not of the book or essay description, nor of the finer samples displayed from pulpit or platform, but of an every-day use, and well suited for the wear and tear of a rough and homely life — a texture which, woven on the hidden loom of a conscious, if ordinary, experience, does not always result in being either coarse or commonplace.

Martha's mental powers had, as we have already observed, only of late been roused from inactivity to action. She had herself been but a working machine — a washing, scrubbing, and little-noticed country girl, to whom few ideas came beyond the round of her every-day work. And the entrance of the Word which giveth understanding unto the simple had set so many new thoughts, so many wonderful bright glimpses of fresh truth revolving in her mind, and arranging themselves as if to be wrought out into some settled scheme, and plain and tangible web of feeling and belief, that she found herself constantly occupied in the determined production for her own satisfaction of this private mungo, all, as soon as spun, laid up in mental store-chambers previously little used, with a sort of surprise that there should be so many things seen and unseen around her, concerning which it behoved her to meditate and take concern.

And now, as through the Norfolk flats the train made its ways, much of this work was in process of being carried on. Home remembrances, and wonderings concerning the now impending future "down at London," and thoughts of Mrs. Estridge's pleasant face and kindly voice, and curious observations concerning the new sensations of real travelling, were so much raw material for Martha's mental "home-spun;" and intermixed with it all was a longing desire to let her life — the new chapter of which was now beginning — be in some sort a return for the Life once given for her, and a dim idea that things here in general were like a journey, and that at last it will not much matter whether we were rich or poor, first-class or third-class passengers — if only we come to the right end and the true home.

Thus Martha went on her way; and gazed out at Ipswich steeples and towers, wondering that there should be so many of them, and making sure that she was not passing London by mistake by inquiring from her fellow-passengers concerning the large station, who laughed at her in a good-natured fashion, and supposed she was new to that line — which was indeed the truth. And, just about the time that Miss Graham, in her corner of the train, had recourse to a nice little luncheon of cold pheasant, and plum-cake, and claret, Martha bethought her of finding occupation of the same sort, and enjoyed her dinner of bread and cheese and apples, which Kezia had put up for her before she left home.

The Eastern Counties line from Winthrop to London has not the merit of being at any point particularly attractive. On the contrary, an observant traveller might very generally be led to suppose it a sort of advertising medium along which, during many months of the year, samples of British fog of various thickness are hung out on approbation, and for general inspection. First come the damps from the Norfolk fens — Martha's native commodity; then the mists from the Orwell, thick and steamy when the tide is out; and later, vapors, more or less dense, from the Essex marshes, hanging like draperies over the telegraph wires, and blocking out all scenery beyond, until the gradual entrance within the regions of genuine London fog, of texture more closely woven, and altogether with a great deal more body in it. And when, through the darkness of the winter afternoon, the train threaded its way to the platform of Bishopsgate Street, and Martha was told that there she was at last, she grasped her bundle with a feeling of companionship in its possession, and got out on to the platform, realizing a sensation of bewilderment and forlornness which momentarily increased with her first experiences of loneliness in a crowd.

The only thing that looked home-like was Miss Graham's face, as she stood chatting to a lady and gentleman who had come to meet her, and to whose carriage — the same to which the Squire had referred on the Winthrop platform — her wraps and lighter appurtenances were being transferred by Green and a footman in attendance; and Martha watched her with as much interest as if she were a picture in a story-book, until she was handed into the carriage, and covered up with what the cottage girl thought looked like skins of wild beasts such as she had seen in a caravan that had once passed through Winthrop, and, telling Green to follow in a cab with the luggage, was driven out of sight.

"I wish there was a wheelbarrow, or something in my line, to meet me," thought Martha; at which moment she was touched on the shoulder by a respectable middle-aged man, who inquired whether she was the young girl down from Norfolk for Mrs. Purkiss; "because, if you are," he added, "I'm her husband, come on purpose to meet you." Whereupon Martha's care was lightened, and she followed him as he carried her bundle to an omnibus outside, and, having arrived at a point of bewilderment beyond which it was impossible to attain, sat in her place awaiting what might happen next, with a general hope that it would all come right.

I believe that in a narrative constituted according to the orthodox fashion, it would be proper here to say,—"And while Martha is pursuing her way along the streets of the metropolis, we will inform our readers who Mrs. Parkiss is." For I have a remembrance that in approved story-books of our childhood, similar occasion for a break in the history were with such pleasant formula made use of for purposes of fresh introductions. "But then," as in thoughtful moments I was inclined to argue, "I can't see what the first person's journey has to do with the other person's history being explained, because it's only in a story after all;" and therefore, resenting any contrivance bearing a resemblance of fictitious unreality, I became immediately impatient of the interruption as being created and made use of under false pretences.

Nevertheless, without reference to our Winthrop maiden's omnibus drive, and subsequent walk through sundry streets under her conductor's protection, I may here mention that Mrs. Purkiss was second cousin to Martha's mother, and that having married many years before, and having " done well for herself," as her family expressed it, in her marriage, she was willing, with just a very little love of patronage, mingled with a great deal of brisk kindliness, to stretch out her hands to less fortunate members of the family, and, in Mrs. Brooke's behalf, to act as a sort of agent for getting her daughters out in situations. Thus had she done for Eliza; thus had she also done for Jane; and thus was she about to do for Martha; " and for the rest, too, as long as I can," she had said to her husband; " for there's always some more of them coming on, and though poor and in a lowly line, they're strong working girls without show or nonsense, as'll do well if they're put right at the first start, which I'm glad to do for them."

And when Martha came in at the private door, escorted by Mr. Purkiss, his wife gave her a friendly welcome, and asked her what she thought of London, and on receiving her first impressions to the effect that it was very big, replied that so she had thought herself when she had come up first, thirty years ago; "but you see, I've come not to think much of it now," she added; while Martha wondered at the greatness of an experience which could speak or even think lightly of so vast and fearful a metropolis as that in which she found herself swallowed up.

And then she had a comfortable cup of tea in the back parlor with her new friends, and was questioned by Mrs. Purkiss concerning all the members of her family in a kind and not too condescending manner, and heard news of her sisters' latest movements,— that Lizzie, she was away at Notting-hill, miles and miles off; and that Jane, she was with her family down at Bloomsbury; but "some day, they'd get a holiday, and Martha should come too, and they'd have tea and buttered toast in this very parlor;" at which pleasant little prospect Mrs. Purkiss grew quite merry, and Martha.

strange and shy as she felt, brightened into an idea that it would be a very high festival indeed.

"And I've got a place for you, Martha, all ready, so you see you won't be like goods on hand and spoiling in keeping," chirruped her second cousin once removed, as she poured out another cup of tea. "It's a stirring sort of place, with plenty of work, and you won't have the grass growing under your feet; but then, as I said to Mr. Purkiss there, and you know he's your cousin too, after a fashion, through me, and my marrying him — as I said to him, 'She's had so much fields and meadows down at Winthrop, why, she won't *want* to let the grass grow here in London;'" whereupon the whole party laughed very much, feeling that this was, as it was intended to be, a very pleasant and amusing view of the matter.

"It's Mrs. Banks, that lets in lodgings down at Southwark," continued Mrs. Purkiss; "I don't know her; but Mrs. Johnson, that's the baker's wife in John Street (it's funny,

Johnson, in John Street, isn't it?), well, she had a cousin that lodged there once, and heard a girl was wanted; and through mentioning it to me, I sent word to say you was coming up, and it'd be the very thing for you: five pounds a year to begin with, and everything found, which isn't bad for a first start."

If Martha had been told by Mrs. Purkiss that she was to go as head chambermaid at Buckingham Palace, on fifty pounds a year board wages, she would have believed that it was all right, and would have proceeded to her destination with a general hope that doing what she was told, and working hard at whatever might be in hand, would carry her through her duties. She had come to a sort of inward conclusion that she was in the world to be directed by somebody, and to work under any person in authority over her, with but a vague idea of distinctions in service; and she was willing to accommodate herself to the circumstances in which she might be placed without troubling her mind much as to what they might be, thus leaving the morrow to its own cares in a manner which many wiser persons find to be far less easy of attainment.

In the course of the evening, being left alone, Mrs. Purkiss informed her young cousin that her husband was a painter and glazier and general decorator. "You've no idea what he can do, my dear," she said; "or rather what he can't do that's at all in his line."

Martha thought she ought to say something, and asked if he built churches.

"Well, no, not exactly *build* them," replied the lady, drawing a basket of stockings towards her, and setting to work at them; "though if we were out at Robinson Crusoe's island, my dear, and wanted one, I shouldn't wonder if he'd build as good a one as any man; though, if you come to think of it," she continued, carrying on the train of thought suggested, "we'd hardly want anything on a large scale out there, a cave or anything else handy would be all one as good as a church; that's what I say; and better than us has had worse praying-places in the world. But in anything to do with windows or pipes, or painter's work, there's no one to make mention of by his side." And then Mrs. Purkiss regaled Martha with a very enthusiastic little sketch of her husband's employments, especially in what she called the decorating department. "He'll explain to you all the outside of the shop tomorrow morning, my dear, which being a corner, is handy for showing off his taste on two sides of the house. He did the same for Lizzy and for Jane, and I know he'll do it for you, especially for my asking; and it's fair you should have a bit of pleasuring before going to your service." And then Mrs. Purkiss hinted that, " if Government knew what was what, they'd have thought of Purkiss along of the Houses of Parliament being got up ornamentally; but there, my dear, we can't expect to take the rule into our hands, however much we think we could improve matters."

Martha's honest conviction as she listened and endeavored to follow out Mrs. Purkiss in her train of thought, was to the effect that if Government, whoever he might be, would take her into counsel and give her a general management of matters, it would be a very good plan indeed, and she went so far as to say so. But Mrs. Purkiss shook her head with a little well-satisfied self-disparagement, saying, "Ah, no, my dear; I might have thought so once perhaps; but, there, you see, I'm not so young as I was; and Purkiss, why he's content for himself, and so I ought to be for him. But here in London there seems to be every one rising one at the top of another in all lines; and there's few know as well as I do the gifts that I tell him he shouldn't hide from the generation that we're called to live in."

Then Martha was silent, and wondered whether, in the line of servants, girls-of-all-work wanted to rise one on the top of the other, and how they managed it, if they did; and soon after, her hostess thought she must be tired, and showed her the very small chamber off the stairs where she was to sleep, and left her saying pleasantly that she'd have to begin London life with a good night, and that Lizzie and Jane too had formerly so started in their respective careers in that identical chamber.

Martha was in truth so very sleepy, that her ideas melted into one another in a very disorderly fashion. She could hardly believe that it was only that morning that she had left home, it seemed such a long, long time ago, almost in a different existence. And then she wondered whether they felt odd without her, and especially whether Mrs. Estridge had been thinking of her as she had promised; and then she thought what a wonderful place London was, and wondered how all the people found enough to eat, when, down at Winthrop, where there were so few, it was often hard to obtain a sufficiency for the poor. And with all this came thoughts, with her evening prayer, concerning the Unspeakable Gift; and she half fancied that it would be easier to remember it, and to live the true life of a pilgrim to heaven, if, instead of travelling in a train, and seeing gas-lights, and being a maid-of-all-work in London, she could dwell in tents and be a shepherdess like

Rachel and Rebekah, in the old days of the world's history. By which time Martha's eyes had grown so heavy, as to be unable to keep open any longer, and she fell asleep with a last remembrance of how comfortable and pretty Miss Graham had looked when she drove away from the station that afternoon, and with the words in her mind, "but after all it'll be the same whether we go first class or third class, if only we get rightly to the journey's end at last."

## CHAPTER IV.

### NO. 19, MILL STREET, SOUTHWARK.

THE next morning, Mr. Purkiss fulfilled his wife's injunction to show Martha the many glories of his external decorations; and she was as much struck with their general aspect as he could possibly have desired.

"This side, you see's devoted to coloring," he observed, leading the way round the corner, and pointing to where, in large squares, somewhat as if designed for a huge chessboard, blue and green and red and orange patches of color were displayed with great brilliancy. "Looks pretty well, doesn't it?" And Martha said she thought it was very beautiful indeed.

"You haven't much of that sort of thing down at your parts, I suppose?" continued Mr. Purkiss, with a little artistic consciousness of merit.

"Oh no," Martha said, "nothing half so fine." Indeed, the only thing she could at all mention that would bear comparison with such glories, was the colored glass in the windows of the church at Winthrop, which she knew Mr. Estridge thought highly of, and which the clerk had said was written about somewhere in a book. But then the colors weren't nearly so bright or plain to see as the squares on Mr. Purkiss's side wall.

"This is the finer kind of work, here in the front," he continued, with increased confidence and friendliness. "You take notice, there's hardly a word in all that, *Purkiss, Painter, Plumber, Glazier, and General Decorator*, which is written in the same letters. That's Roman, and the next old English, and the next Italics, and so on; and you see it's all worked into a scroll, which is a fancy of mine for use and ornament both. It's not every one," he went on, "who can see the thought and feeling of my line of life. There's Vawse, now, he's something in the same business, being a plumber, though I take to the decorating most myself. Well, I met him after the last frost, going about quite in a low way. 'Ah, Purkiss,' he says, 'everything seems to go against us this year.' 'Why, how so?' I asked of him, though knowing what he was after as well as most.

"'Why,' he says, 'this here frost, I looked to its going off all of a sudden, and pipes giving way all round the neighborhood, and flooding of houses, and we being called up like doctors in the night, and paid accordingly. And now it's all thawed so gradual, like anyone sinking by inches; and I've not heard of a pipe burst anywhere round, excepting one of my own, which is all loss and no gain.'

"'Vawse,' I said to him, 'feel that — feel it if you must, and I feel it too, for we're all mortal; but don't say it. It lowers a profession for a man that's in it to be giving of it out that he thrives on other folks' trials and cares, which, though they must come, and we wouldn't, even for their good, wish it otherwise, is trouble still. A doctor doesn't give out that he's low in spirits because of a healthy season, though he may have a wife and family like you, and feelings with them such as yours; and it's unbecoming for you and me to act in any way different in the matter.' That's what I said to him."

Martha intimated that she was sure he was very kind; and then Mrs. Purkiss called them in to breakfast, and asked her what she thought of all that she had seen, and agreed with her that it would take a great deal to go beyond her husband's success in the outward coloring of their abode.

And then, after the cups and saucers had been cleared away, Martha collected her things once more into the old shawl bundle, and Mr. Purkiss, who had business in Southwark, took her in charge; and, after grateful good-byes to his good-natured wife, she walked silently by his side through many and various streets, wondering much that he should always know which way to turn; and was finally left by him on the door-steps of No. 19, Mill Street, which, she was told, was to be her new abode.

In the lives of great people and of small people there are moments, standing out always in after memories, in which one's personal identity forms the sole link of connection between different chapters in one's individual history, and which intervening between a completely finished past and a completely unknown future, are looked back upon as moments never to be forgotten. Martha, as she stood on the door-step in Mill Street, remained still for a moment, realizing that, with the retreating form of Mr. Purkiss, her last link to the old life amongst kith and kin was cut. She would be no longer Martha Brooke amongst those with whom she might be thrown, but simply "the girl." She was on the brink of an altogether new existence, and there was a little fear concerning it in her heart.

Some readers will possibly think that an unusually small amount of care and thought had been expended upon her settlement in London, and that the speedy arrangement for her services in the house of a stranger betrayed an absence of concern on the part of her relations, not often encountered even in Martha's line of life. Little do such readers — possibly the Miss Grahams of our social circles, cared for, guarded, protected in all their ways, and in all their comings and goings, from possible and impossible annoyances or anxieties — know the absolute recklessness with which young ignorant country sisters are cast upon the perilous seas of London life to sink or swim, with no arm outstretched by friend or protector to hold them up in the dangerous waters.

In comparison with the majority of girls similarly sent forth, Martha was ushered into her new position with an extraordinary amount of protection; and Mrs. Purkiss, in having made inquiry of Mrs. Johnson, who further made inquiry of her cousin, concerning the respectability of Mrs. Banks and her lodging-house, and in having satisfied herself that

"Eliza Brooke's girl would be in safe keeping, and have no chance of bad company," had performed the office of protectress, as a good angel of discretion, and in a manner which too few allow themselves to regard as a necessity, and which fully justified Mrs. Brooke's announcements to Winthrop neighbors, that "she had friends in London such as finer folks might be glad on, and that there wasn't nothing common about the way *her* girls was got out once they were off her hands."

And if a line might here be written on behalf of a race comparatively neglected, and yet so numerous as to be altogether beyond estimation: a race, concerning which pages and volumes might record the sad story, "No man cared for my soul," it would be to entreat a word of encouragement, of solicitude, of help for the often overtasked serving sister whose country home is an old story with her now, and who has been cast adrift upon a life to which but scant rays of sunshine find their way — a word which may wake up tender thoughts of the past and some hopes for the future, if truly spoken for His sake who once took upon Himself the form of a servant, and who even now bids us by love serve one another.

Martha had not stood for more than a moment on the doorstep before she became conscious that a storm of wrath was going forward within; and the sudden opening of the door, from which a girl of about her own size hastily came forth into the street, suggested to her that it might probably be the best opportunity for presenting herself to her new employer.

Within stood a stout middle-aged woman, who, being charged with a priming of words, originally, and in the commencement of delivery, intended for the outgoing damsel, seemed to consider that it might be an unnecessary economy to reserve the remainder for Martha at a more distant moment; so that the first sentence which greeted the Winthrop maiden was the general remark, —

"And you call yourself a servant by the name of Hannah Jane, and throwing out crumbs for birds from out of the table-cloth into the yard, which, browned in the oven, would have come in for the front parlor's fish this very day. It's a good thing you're going, or I'd Hannah Jane you, and any one else that has ways of that sort in this house."

At the conclusion of which observation, or rather during a pause in which Mrs. Banks seemed to be considering what she should say next, she allowed herself to become suddenly aware of Martha's presence, and stopped to say,—

"O, I suppose you're the girl!"

Martha replied, timidly, that she thought she was.

"You might have come an hour sooner, then," was the rejoinder, "for all that's to be got through of work before dinner-time; and I hope that you've hands and feet, and a mind to use the same, which is more than most girls has now-a-days."

Martha hoped she had, but hardly ventured to say so; and after this brief introduction, her new mistress led the way to a sort of large cupboard looking over the leads at the top of the house, wherein was room for a rough bed and a stool, telling her she might leave her bundle there, and come down, as soon as she had put on her working-clothes, to the kitchen, where abundance of work was in store for her.

Mrs. Banks, as our readers will already have discovered, was not a woman of gentle disposition. The cares of a London life, and still more the care of a London lodging-house, do not tend to soften a hard temper, and tend very much indeed to the hardening of a rough one. She was not naturally harsher than many others of her class; but having grown up as the daughter of a letter of lodgings, and having pursued the same calling in later life, she had seen a great deal of the worst side of men and women, had found out that people sometimes go off without remembering to pay just and lawful claims, that the grocer occasionally puts sand into the sugar, and the baker alum into the bread; that servants now and then have tendencies to dawdle or to go out when they should remain within, and that the collectors of rates and taxes are frequent in their calls, and never forget the number of the house. And so it had come to be that, with Mrs. Banks, eyes and ears and tongue had formed themselves into a sort of defence committee against the ways of the outer world, and that, unhappily for her own peace of mind, her plan had come to be that of believing every one to be guilty unless, by some rarely-returned verdict, proved to be the reverse. In her eyes there were three great divisions of society,—a king, lords, and commons, into which all that portion of mankind resolved itself which lay within her ken — parlors, two-pair fronts, and attics. And it was concerning this threefold apportionment that Martha was, at her first outset in service, duly enlightened.

It seemed to her, on that first day, as if she were fighting and struggling against a whirlwind of "what's to be done next?" as if cooking and cleaning, and washing-up, and answering bells, and trying to remember orders from Mrs. Banks, followed one upon the other with a fierce and bewildering confusion; as if she had never known real weariness before; while at the same time she felt half guilty at being so tired, since her mistress seemed gifted with powers of "following round" which were not exhausted by the close of the evening.

She wanted to remember the names and places of a hundred things which were new to her, and, above all, the directions for her future conduct to the lodgers, which Mrs. Banks showered down upon her rapidly.

"You mind — whatever comes, the front parlor's before all when it rings. The door may wait, but never the parlor. They pay reg'lar, and they expect reg'lar service, which attendance and linen is named in the agreement; and I'm never going to lose good lodgers for idle servants. Two-pair fronts, now, may wait. If it comes handy, I don't mind your looking in, but I wouldn't have such as them giving of themselves airs, or taking out in attendance, besides their paying of sixpence less than those who was there before them."

"And suppose the other people, up at the top, ring too?" inquired Martha, somewhat timidly; "mustn't I go to them?"

Mrs. Banks looked at her new handmaiden for a moment in speechless surprise, holding up the toasting-fork which she had at that instant in her hand as a sort of visible and incorporate note of exclamation at the audacity of the idea which her question suggested.

"Top attics ring!" she exclaimed, after fully taking in the idea, "top attics ring — ring bells and paying two shillings a week for one room, kitchen fire not included. I fancy I hear them. I'd attic them pretty soon, I can tell you;" whereupon Martha was willing to let the subject drop as speedily as possible, while her mistress murmured to herself all the way up-stairs at the suggestion which had for a moment, as she expressed it, "most taken away her breath."

It will have been perceived by the reader that Mrs. Banks had invented a mode of defence in her conflict with the world which admitted of very extensive use in the way of warfare. It was simply that of adopting as a threatening weapon the last noun of importance which had been used by herself or the object of her wrath, and which by being, as it were, picked up from the field of battle, and winged and barbed for use by transposition into an active verb, was launched forth from her lips with a vague and terrible indefiniteness of meaning which, in inexperienced ears, added greatly to its power and effect. It was after an account of the misdemeanors of the last servant who had been known on one occasion to "overlay herself," as Mrs. Banks expressed it, until seven o'clock in the morning, and with the added reminiscence, "I seven o'clocked her pretty well, I can tell you," that Martha at last found her way to her sleeping chamber. She had it to herself, at least for the present; though her mistress had forewarned her that "as likely as not she'd have to give it up to some one as would pay for it, and make up a bed for herself in the back-kitchen, which she hoped she might never find herself worse off, and a good blanket on the bed that had cost her twelve and six a pair, if it had cost a penny."

And when Martha had sat down for a minute on her bed to rest and think, she went to the little garret window in the roof, and, in spite of the cold, opened it and looked out. The keen frost had given place to a milder temperature; but the stars were shining up above the fog and smoke as they had shone two days before above the damps of the Norfolk fens; and the crescent moon was high and bright over the great city as she had seen it from among the grave-stones in Winthrop Church-yard on the Christmas afternoon which seemed now so long ago.

Martha was tired in body and mind; and the sense of being swallowed up as a drop in the great ocean of London life gave her a feeling of depression and bewilderment.

"So many chimneys," she said to herself, looking over the wilderness of house-tops spreading out on every side — "so many chimneys, and every chimney going down to some place, and every place full of people.

It seems like being lost among such crowds. I wonder if there's maids-of-all-work in all the houses that's got to be followed round and worked hard like me. I wonder whether they'll be thinking of me at home, which is so far off as if one would never get there again. Mother used to scold, but somehow it seems harder to take when one's to take wages with it, and meaning well all the time. I wonder whether Mrs. Estridge will keep her promise to think of me. I think of her all sorts of times, but it's so different for a lady like her; and she doesn't know how lost one seems away from every-one, and in such a big place that I wouldn't know my way back for any money. I wonder what Miss Graham's doing now — somewhere in London too. I'd like to meet her or see her go by; — it'd be something from Winthrop.

"But I must try and do right, and be true. I remember how Mrs. Estridge said once 'He calleth the stars by their names.' There's lots of them up there — as many as there is people in London; but He calls them all right, and it says there's not one faileth. And then she said He calls *us* by name, and we find grace in His sight. I wish I could remember everything as well as all that she said that afternoon after Mary Lee was buried; but I'll ask Him to call me by name — like His own sheep — when I'm put about or tired or dull — to let me feel His voice as she said He would; and — "

But Martha's reflections were interrupted by the striking of the hour from towers and steeples which stood out in the fog and moonlight like guardians of the city while it slept. The news of the departure to give in its account of another hour, was proclaimed in different tones — slowly and solemnly on one side, lightly and hurriedly on others; here, heavily, and as if laden with the burden of the world's weariness, and there with a jaunty attempt at seeming not to care about the matter. And before the last tone had died away, a sweet voice of chimes seemed to bring a farewell message of hope and greeting from the parting hour as it sped — chimes like those of Winthrop Church, and which brought the same tears to Martha's eyes which had filled them when Mrs. Estridge's hand had been on her shoulder and her voice in her ears.

"It's to remind me — it's to make me remember 'the Unspeakable Gift,'" she said to herself, with a sudden springing up of thought and desire in her heart. "I won't forget — I won't ever give way if I can help it, or think He doesn't mind about me because I'm common and only a plain servant. I'll try, O, I'll try and please Him, because He came for me. Those bells will remind me when I forget, and I'm so glad they're here. And I'll keep the Christmas chimes going on in my heart — as the message said — like it went to Winthrop bells on Christmas-day — yes, it's thanks be unto God for His Unspeakable Gift — that's the chime I'll keep always going."

## CHAPTER V.

MARTHA AND THE TOP ATTIC MAKE FRIENDS.

ARTHA had not been many days in Mrs. Banks' employment before she observed that, early every morning, after having duly cleaned and set to rights the top attic mentioned by her mistress as being charged two shillings a week, kitchen fire not included, a careworn and elderly woman came forth, as for a day's work, never returning until six o'clock in the evening, at which time she carried with her a small basket apparently containing whatever marketings she had been able to procure. Martha thought she had distinguished the sound of voices in the room, but never from morning till night having a

moment to herself, she had only been able to wonder who the other occupant of the chamber might be.

All she knew was that the name was Elmhurst, and that bearers of that name were thought of but slightingly by Mrs. Banks, who uttered a general intimation that she would "pretty soon attendance anyone who dawdled about top attics when there was parlors wanted looking after," and who took good care that the provision of down-stair work should be sufficient to prevent any such transgression, had Martha been so inclined.

Sunday came — the first Sunday she had ever passed away from Winthrop — and with it Martha had hoped for a little quiet. She did not mind work; on the contrary, she rather liked to get through creditably with the cleaning and cooking and polishing that followed so rapidly one upon the other; and although there was something rather alarming in her first waiting at table for such particular persons as Mrs. and Miss Smythe, who were "the parlors" in Mrs. Banks' establishment, and who held themselves high, and did not condescend to speak to the servant, still she made up with strength and willingness for what she wanted in experience. There were two things, however, for which Martha was unconsciously longing. The first was for an interval — if only an hour — of quiet; and the other, for the sound — if only for a few minutes — of a friendly voice. She did not know the name of a feeling that was over her — a feeling of longing and heart-yearning and sadness, such as she had never felt before, but which came to her at night before she went to sleep, and by day, when hands and feet were busy in kitchen and wash-house, and constantly when the chimes from the friendly steeple reminded her of Winthrop, and of little Mary Lee in the churchyard — a strange heart-hunger, which you and I may have felt and known as home-sickness. For do not imagine, my reader, that those who have left happy homes, and who know that they are followed by the prayers of loving parents and fond sisters, and who can in fancy hear tender voices blended in remembrances of the absent one, are the only ones to whom home-sickness comes. Far from it. The wanderer from many a home, as hard and loveless as the Brookes' cottage on the fens — the ragged boy, who has never had a father's house — may yet in secret heart-chambers know that inner craving for something to which no word answers but home; and I have sometimes thought that the need of an abiding resting-place for the heart, and of a sure centre for our unspoken affections and desires, is shadowed forth in the longings which we call home-sickness, whether here it be satisfied or not.

Martha was home-sick, more because she missed having something familiar, something by right belonging to her, than because she could look back to any endearing associations in her own family; and more, far more, with the longing in her heart for Mrs. Estridge's face and voice, than for anything else in all Winthrop. And on this first Sunday she had felt as if she would like to find her way to the church with the chimes, as if it would be like finding a friend — a friend telling her about "the Unspeakable Gift;" and so, though with some misgivings, as to how her petition would be received, she had asked Mrs. Banks whether, after washing up breakfast things and tidying the rooms, she would be able to let her go to church.

If Martha had indulged in some fears concerning the matter, they were fully justified by Mrs. Banks, who seemed to think that for a servant-of-all-work to ask to go to church in the morning was a beginning which might lead to heights of presumption to which no imagination would enable her to follow.

"Church! You receiving of five pounds a-year, tea and sugar and washing found, or soap given for the last, which there's everything for drying out at the back, — church, this time of the day, when the parlors has a gentleman to dinner, and hot shoulder of mutton coming on the table, and the upstairs' people at home, and calling for boots over the stairs, and you talking, like a lady, of going out to church! Well, Hannah Jane wasn't much, and took mindin' to that extent, that I've told her she'd be best standin' for a sign over the house-door, like the Chinaman with a tail, and a canister in his hand, over the tea store, the other side of the way, for all the good she was in the house — Hannah Jane wasn't much, but she'd have thought twice before she brought it up to me about church-going, though I let her go out twice a month in the evenings to church or chapel, or anything that came handy, which is more than most would, and don't care if you do the same, so that there's nothing wanting doing at home. You talk to me of church-going again this time of day, and I'll tell you where it'll end; and that's in your expecting of a silk gown, and a carriage to the door, with a double knock, and a footman to carry your book before you, and the clergyman to wait prayers, with everybody looking over their prayer-books to see who it is. You go and clean up those things, or I'll church you pretty soon, I can tell you."

Martha obeyed quite silently, and occupied herself with trying to discover the links by which, from Mrs. Banks' point of view, her desire for church-going would land her at last at that point of her expecting the carriage and the livery-footman, and wondered that people should be so different from each other as her mistress and Mrs. Estridge. And then came the usual week-day hurry and scolding; and if it had not been for the chimes, and for seeing people go by with books in their hands, and for the church-going look about them, and for the closed shops, and for the extra dinner for the first-story people, who, being clerks in an office, stayed at home on that day only, Martha would hardly have known that it was Sunday, or believed that it meant the same as it did at Winthrop.

It was not till the afternoon that she managed to secure a quiet half-hour. Mrs. Banks went out in a grand dress of green silk, put on only for state occasions, leaving many injunctions with her servant as to the lodgers' tea, and as to her own behavior in respect of temptations to look out of the window, and to gossip out of the door, and to find her way out of the area, such as it had not occurred to Martha to think of. And then, when everything had been put away, and for awhile all was still, she went up to her own little room, and, sitting down, began to think of home.

"Just half-past two," she said to herself; "Mrs. Estridge is giving out the hymn now. They'll miss me, I think; at least, she promised she would, and I do believe she meant it. I wonder what she'll be saying to them this afternoon. Oh, I wish, I wish I could be there! It'd be such a help, and I seem to want something to help me. It all seems one day like another here; and though they didn't care for good things at home, there was always Sunday for church and going up to the Bible-class. I wish I had been braver to speak to Mrs. Estridge and tell her that I'm trying to serve Jesus,— that I've asked for the Unspeakable Gift. It seemed so hard to tell her, I was feeling it all deep inside. If only ladies knew how hard it is for poor girls to speak to them, they'd find out it's not always because we don't care.

"And now how am I to keep true and get on? There's no one to speak a word to me here. I can't even get to church regular, and that would have been something. Missus, why she'd scorn me if she was to know I thought He cared for me: and it all seems a life without any one else to care. I'd work hard,—I want to work hard; but I want to remember all the same. I want to please Him,—I want to do everything right for His sake who came at Christmas-time for mine. And oh, if only He'll help me! If only He'll keep me from giving up and not caring. And He says He will. That's what Mrs. Estridge said two Sundays ago: 'I am poor and needy, but the Lord careth for me.' And then He's pleased if we try to do what He tells us. It says so in the Bible. And I'll try,—I will; I think I am trying. I'll not answer back, and I'll do all my work as well as I can; and I'll thank Him for caring to think about me in this great big place, and I only a stupid plain servant, with nobody else to mind how I get on."

Then Martha read a little out of her Winthrop Bible, and knelt down, and asked Jesus Christ, the Saviour, of Bethlehem, to help her to be true, and in her little humble life to show forth His praise; and she read the Collect prayer for pardon and peace, and asked that she might be cleansed from her sins, and serve Him with a quiet mind, and that though she couldn't go to church, yet that she might feel it was Sunday and keep it holy before Him. And then, when the chimes sounded into her room as with a special Sabbath message, she told Him that she wanted to keep the chimes always going in her heart, — the Christmas chime of thanks for the Unspeakable Gift: and when she rose up, the afternoon sun was streaming into her room, and there was a great peace in the heart of the little maid-of-all-work, and she found herself singing in a low voice, and with a wonderful thankfulness in her soul, the words of the Christmas hymn: —

> "Joyful all ye nations rise,
> Join the triumph of the skies;
> With the heavenly hosts proclaim,
> Christ is born at Bethlehem."

She had only ceased for a minute or two when the handle of the door was turned, and the elderly woman known to inhabit the top attic appeared, dressed, evidently, for afternoon service.

"I'm going to church," she said; "I wish you'd give a look in now and then at my poor girl, and see if she wants anything. I've never had a chance to speak to you before."

Martha came to a rapid conclusion that looking in on a Sunday afternoon need not be counted as the "attendance," so much resented in idea by Mrs. Banks; and knocked at the door as Mrs. Elmhurst went down the stairs.

"Come in," said a weary voice from within; and so invited she entered at once.

The room, poor and scantily furnished as it was, was exquisitely neat; and on a sort of couch made by the extension of an old horsehair mattress upon two rough deal boxes, lay a girl of about eight and twenty, covered with a coarse woollen shawl. There was a look of education and thoughtfulness in her face, which in a moment impressed Martha with respect; while, at the same time, an occasional expression of weariness and anxiety kindled the sympathies which in our Winthrop maiden's case had been repressed by the harshness of her outer life, but had by no means been extinguished.

"You're the new servant, I suppose," said the stranger, taking in at a glance all that showed itself in Martha's appearance of sturdy straightforward homeliness.

"Yes," replied Martha, hardly knowing how to begin advances; "I've been here ever since Wednesday; but I didn't know anything about your being up here."

"It's hardly likely you would," replied the invalid; "we're only top attics," she added, with a half smile; "I hardly think Mrs. Banks knows my name."

"I knew your mother was Elmhurst," said Martha; "but she never spoke to me till to-day, and I didn't dare to look in without asking."

"No one ever does look in," was the answer; "little Hannah, that went away last week, did, now and then, when she had a chance; but she couldn't stand the work. How do you get on?"

Martha said that she got on middling, — it all seemed very strange at first; and Mrs. Banks seemed easily put out. Then she added, by way of excuse, — for certain thoughts belonging to the last hour had made her feelings towards her mistress and every one else gentler than before, — "country ways are different to town ways, I suppose."

"You're from the country, then?" said the sick girl inquiringly; and Martha replied that she was, — that, in fact, she was "out of Norfolk."

"I'm from the country, too," she went on. "My name's Kate — Kate Elmhurst. I used to live away in Somersetshire, down amongst the hills, before father died. I sometimes think I'd give everything in the world to be down in the country again."

"It seems quite different here," rejoined Martha, by way of saying something.

"It's the roar," said Kate; "the roar of the city which never stops. I lie here wondering how it felt to be quite still, — to hear nothing but stillness, — and then I sometimes feel as if I shall go crazy just for a minute's quiet. There's less noise Sundays; but all the same, there's no silence — no quiet."

"Have you been long here?" asked Martha, with a sort of shyness over her on occasion of almost her first visit to a sick bed.

"Two years laid up. Father died five years ago. He was a gardener. And then mother and me thought we'd get on better up here, and she went out to needlework, and I worked at a factory. The people where we lodged at first behaved badly to us, and we got poorer and poorer; and then I was ill and couldn't work; and now mother she keeps on trying to get enough for us both, and brings me a little work when she can get it; but it's only a very little, after all."

"I'm so sorry," said Martha, with true womanly pity coming into her dark grey eyes, "I wish I could do anything for you. What laid you up?"

"Biscuits," was the answer, as Kate wearily changed her position.

"Biscuits!" exclaimed Martha, who endeavored in vain to remember any form of illness of which she had ever heard having biscuits as a symptom.

"Yes; I worked at the biscuit-mills. It was a long way to walk, and I wasn't strong. I think I over-walked very often. My work was among the packers, and though it didn't seem hard to look on at, it was hard for me. I was at it from seven in the morning till six in the evening. The people weren't unkind to me, but it was the stooping all day in the hot room, full of people and noise, that seemed to tire me out. Then mother was taken ill, and I sat up with her all night. I couldn't afford to be with her by day, for my six shillings a week was all we had to live on. And then when she got better, I was taken ill, and they said it was my back, and I know they said I'd never get well again. I was very ill at first, and a sort of fever came on me, and by times I was delirious. And all through I never seemed to see anything but biscuits. Every noise was biscuits mixing, or being poured out over me, or weighing for the tins and not coming right. I used to think I was packing and couldn't get them into the boxes; or hungry, and couldn't get anything to eat but biscuits; or, worse still, thirsty, and they'd give me biscuits instead of water. I hope I'll never have such a time again. When I got better, I found I couldn't get about, and mother got this room cheap, and she has to work for both of us."

Martha listened with deepest interest. "It must have been dreadful," she said; and then, with a sudden expression of sympathy, of which in her shyness she almost felt ashamed, she added, "it must feel so long lying here all day."

"Yes, it does," said Kate — "very long. I hear you stirring, and going up and down stairs, and I try to remember what it feels like to get about. I know nearly all that goes on by putting things together — footsteps, and knocks at the door, and bells ringing, and

Mrs. Banks calling out on the stairs, and the other people's voices; and then I think how much strength there is in the world — how many people that can walk about without ever troubling to think of it — while I'm obliged to see mother work for us both. That's the hardest of all to bear. She's getting old, and it's heavy for her, though I'm not much to keep. And then I seem to long for some one to come in and say a word to me while she's out. I've been wondering what sort you were; and just now I heard you singing, all quiet to yourself, a bit of a hymn like we had at our home in the country, and I said to mother, Ask her to come in."

Martha's eyes glistened with pleasure. "It's what we had at my home in the country on Christmas-day — only last Tuesday," she said. "O, I wish you knew Winthrop, and our church and Mrs. Estridge — she'd come to see you, and you'd like her ever so much."

"They say there's a district lady comes round here," said Kate. "Hannah told me so; but Mrs. Banks doesn't care for her coming in. Hannah said that once she only called out to her from the back stairs, 'Nothing to-day, thank you,' just as if she'd been a tradesperson; and that she told her she needn't mind leaving books, as she hadn't time to read them. I wish district ladies would ask for the lodgers. I asked Hannah to beg her to come up to me; but she was afraid of her mistress' scolding her."

"I'll ask her to come up," said Martha, with the first sudden resolution that she had ever made in her mind. "I daresay it can be managed; and Kate, I'd like to look in now and then — just when I'm going by, and do up your fire, and tell you what I'm about. I'm so sorry for you," she added.

Kate looked as if the sympathy of the new visitor was very pleasant to her. "I'll tell you what I'd like you to do now," she said; "I'd like you to sing that Christmas hymn to me, I used to sing in the choir in our church at home, and to deck it up with holly and ivy; and then we used to have hymns and carols up at the Rectory. I think of it now sometimes when the time comes round; and O, Martha, do you know I'm sometimes rebellious. You don't know what it's like to see mother work for me, or to think that if things had been different, I might have kept well and strong. I used to read tracts about sick people, and now, do you know, they sometimes make me worse. Those in the tracts are always good, and always happy, and say they don't feel lonely, and that they wouldn't be well again if they could; and I'm quite different. I'd give everything in the world to be well again. I think of it all day. Waking in the morning's the worst — waking up to know that I can't get up — that every day'll be the same till I die, unless mother dies first, and then I'll go to the workhouse. I'd like a book about people who are ill and can't get about, and are longing to get well again."

Martha hardly knew what to say, so she set to work at remembering the Christmas hymn, and Kate took up the tune with a soft sweet second, as far as the words

"Life and light to all He brings,
Shines with healing in His wings."

Then her voice faltered, as she recalled the country days of her childhood, and the church in which she had formerly sung them, and she whispered out, — " But there's not the life and light and healing to me, Martha."

Martha didn't know what to say. The tears were up in her own eyes, as she sat on the floor by Kate's couch. At last, however, the silence was broken by the sound of the chimes, pouring in as with comforting voice for the weary girl lying there in her sorrow.

" They're just like ours used to be at Ockley Coombe," she said, seeing that Martha kindled at the sound.

" And they're just like ours at Winthrop," echoed her companion joyfully; and then, as if with a new thought, she told Kate about Mrs. Estridge, and about the Unspeakable Gift, and about Mary Lee, and about the message in the letter, and how they were to keep the Christmas chime always going in their hearts, and about how she thought that Jesus would help them to do it if they tried.

" And do you keep it going?" asked Kate

—"here with all your work to do, and Mrs. Banks after you all day?"

"I try — at least, I want to try," was Martha's somewhat timid reply. "I'm sure we can, if He helps us."

"It's easier for people who can get about," said Kate, wearily; "I could, perhaps, if I was strong again. I know about it. Mother's a Christian. She prays by me every night, and leaves me the Bible to read every morning. I was confirmed, and I thought I was a Christian too; but when I can't feel to say, 'Thy will be done,' I think I'm not. And yet — and yet — Martha, I long to feel the Unspeakable Gift like mother does; and I pray here, when I'm all alone, for God to help me. Sometimes I think if I was in the country again, and still, I could be more willing; and at night sometimes, when I can't sleep, and when I hear all the roar of the city, I look up where the stars are, and I think it's all country up there — it's all quiet and still up in the sky — the smoke and noise of the world can't get up there. And a sort of peace comes into my heart, thinking that He's there, and that He'll care. But that's only now and then," she added, wearily, " and then I'm as bad as ever."

"It must be very hard," said Martha again; " and yet —"

" Well; and yet what?"

" Why, if you *could* keep the chime going too, and thank Him in your heart, it seems to me as if — as if He'd be so pleased. It'll be better than mine, for He must know how much harder it is for sick people. I can fancy He'd like it as much as the angels' music, and it would be such a great thing for you to be doing it up here — keeping it going in your heart all by yourself."

Martha felt quite ashamed at having said more than she had ever said in her life of what was in her thoughts. But the true woman's nature of sympathy and tenderness had been drawn out in her by the sight of weariness and sickness; and, moreover, her separation from home, her being cut off from the help and encouragement which she had previously known, to fight her way amongst strangers, had done more in a few days to bring out independence of thought and action than had years of her quiet Winthrop life. She sat quite still by Kate's side, wishing that she could be a comforter to her in her trouble, until the warning sound of Mrs. Banks' voice, as she returned from her visits, roused her to her feet.

But as she wished her new friend good-bye, there was a look of more rest in Kate's face than there had been at the first, and she returned the farewell with the words, "I'll try too, Martha. We'll both try together to keep the chime going in our hearts — the Christmas chime. You look in, and remind me now and then, that I may try and say always, 'Thanks be unto God for His Unspeakable Gift.' I believe it's a step to saying, 'Thy will be done.'"

## CHAPTER VI.

### MARTHA FINDS THE COALS HEAVIER.

SOLOMON said truly that "a continual dropping in a very rainy day and a contentious woman are alike;" but, if I had my choice, I would of the two very much prefer the rainy day.

I think Martha would have preferred it too; for, hard as she worked, and earnestly as she endeavored to do her best, Mrs. Banks seemed to persist in the belief that she had on hand a perpetual design of wrong-doing, and that nothing but a ceaseless succession of scoldings and threatenings on her part would in anywise prevail to keep her handmaiden from breaking dishes, gossipping with the milkman, purloining remains of repasts belonging to the front parlors, neglecting her duties in cleaning and dusting, and, in fact, from committing any misdemeanors into which she could possibly be led astray.

Still the weeks passed on; and it was not until she had been for three or four months in London that Martha began to wonder why she always felt tired. It seemed so odd, she thought; and she wished that it wasn't so hard to get up in the morning, and fancied that the coals must be of a heavier sort than the first, only, then, the water couldn't have grown heavier too.

During these weeks she had been several times to church in the evening, Mrs. Elmhurst having come forward in her behalf, and promised to see to the lodgers' suppers, if Martha might be spared. And she had gone to the church with the chimes, and had felt home-like and happy as the well-known words were spoken, and the psalm sung, which she liked best of all, in which it says, "With His own right hand and with His holy arm hath He gotten Himself the victory."

And, one evening, the festival shadowed forth in promise by Mrs. Purkiss on her first night in London, came to pass; and Eliza from Notting-hill, and Jane from her situation in Bloomsbury, came to tea at the house of the general decorator's hospitable little wife, and were regaled, as promised, with buttered toast, and with many other good things. And though Mrs. Banks at first steadily refused to give Martha an evening out, yet, when Mrs. Purkiss herself called to proffer her request, she at last consented — only taking out the indulgence granted to the young maid-of-all-work in a double indulgence of her own tongue, and winding up her scolding over Martha's first breakage with the frequent threat, " Talk of going out to tea-parties, I'll tea-party you if I have you coming to me with another glass broken, which it cost sevenpence three farthings, if it cost a penny. You mind, I shall stop it of your quarter's wages the next time you look to be paid."

Martha was well-pleased to see her sisters, and to talk over Winthrop news with them;

and she was rather surprised at finding them so tall, and with an air of experience, and a fearless knowledge of town ways, to which she thought it unlikely she could ever attain. They told her that she was growing thin, and advised her to better herself — an idea which had never for a moment dawned on her mind as a possibility; and she thought of their words very deeply as she walked home; but the remembrance of Kate Elmhurst was quite enough to put such an idea out of her head.

For, indeed, to the invalid girl she had come to be such a help and comfort as she could never have hoped to be to anyone. She could seldom sit with her, except on Sunday afternoons: but daily, and many times a day, she would look in for a moment, make up the fire, arrange her pillows, or speak a brave, cheery word of comfort, which helped Kate to fight her own harder battle — to toil in rowing, though the wind might be contrary, against the waves and breakers which surround the tranquil haven of resignation, over which is the inscription, "Thy will be done."

Yes, Martha was keeping the chime going in her heart, and it filled it more than the sound of Mrs. Banks' voice, or than the roar and turmoil of the great city around her.

Then a great joy had one day come to her — a letter, bearing a Norfolk postmark, and signed "E. Estridge." How Martha's heart throbbed as she read the letter! How she wondered whether anyone in the whole of London could boast of such a prize, and laid it beside her bed at night, and read it when she woke up in the morning! How she showed it to Kate and her mother, and kept a little festival in her heart on occasion of such an accession to her treasures! How trifling appeared the troubles of her everyday life, and Mrs. Banks' scoldings, and the lodgers' impatient rings! Had she not that in her possession which had lit up quite an illumination of joy and pleasure within? Had not Mrs. Estridge — a lady, who had so many to think of — remembered her, Martha Brooke, a poor, awkward maid-of-all-work, and cared for her enough to write her a letter all for herself? Every word, as Martha said to herself, was written expressly for her; she must have thought of her all the time she was writing — all the time, indeed, that " she was making up the letter to write it." How could she be thankful enough, or tell Mrs. Estridge sufficiently what a bank-note of joy it had been to her, or make her a little bit understand, what she would have been far too shy to say in words, that she thought of her and prayed for her day and night; that the remembrance of every word she had ever spoken to her was in her heart; that the thought of those words was helping her on in her fight and in her struggle to be a Christian, even when it was hardest; that to be with her once more was her dearest earthly wish, cherished in the midst of much cleaning and scrubbing by day, and of Winthrop dreams by night.

The letter which so filled Martha's heart with rejoicing was as follows: —

"Winthrop Rectory, March 27.

"Dear Martha,

"I am sure you are often thinking of Winthrop and of all your friends here; and I think it will please you to have a few lines from me, to tell you that we remember you, and talk of you very often too. I was with your mother a few days ago, and she told me that she had heard from you, and that you were in the same place in Southwark to which you went at first; and that you had seen Eliza and Jane, and that they were both well. I am so glad that you have met, for London is such a great city, that I can fancy your feeling a little bit sorrowful and lonely at having no one belonging to you at hand.

"We think of you so often in the Bible class, and I miss your voice in the choir on Sundays, and hope that some day or other, when you get a holiday, I shall have you with me again. I have taken Kezia into the Bible class now, and I think your brother Willy will be able to join the singing-class by-and-bye. I do not think there have been any other changes since you left home. Spring is beginning to appear even in our cold part of the world; and Miss Gracie has just brought me in some violets, of which I send you a few as messengers from Winthrop.

"And now, dear Martha, I must tell you how earnestly I desire for you that, though separated from your friends here, you may feel that the true and unchanging Friend is always near you. I daresay things are not always smooth with you — He often sees it good for us that we should be led in rough paths; but if we give our hands into His, He will show us that He is leading us forth by the right way to the city of habitation. Never be satisfied with just being called a Christian — with merely knowing *about* Christ, instead of knowing him for your own Saviour. It makes everything so different when we think all day long, ' I may do this for Jesus. I may get through my common every-day work well, and with all my heart, to please Him. I may refuse to speak this angry word, because He would not like it.' I find that this thought helps me in my work, and I like to think that you and I are together in trying to serve Him and love Him and please Him, and I hope that we shall be together with Him in heaven. I think I must give you this message before I close:—'To him that overcometh will I give a crown of life.'

"I have only time to say that Mr. Estridge sends you his best wishes, and to remain, dear Martha,

"Your very true friend,

"E. ESTRIDGE."

It was not a long letter, but there was that in it which filled the young servant with surprise and joy. That she and Mrs. Estridge should be together in anything — that she should write as if they two were fighting side by side, shoulder to shoulder, in Jesus Christ's army — seemed quite a fresh spring of happiness. And then those violets! To think of her putting them into the letter, just as if she had been writing to a lady like herself! Winthrop violets, gathered by Miss Grace, and actually sent to her by Mrs. Estridge. The Queen herself, if on terms of correspondence with the Rector's wife (and Martha would not have been at all surprised had this been the case), could not be treated more considerately. The violets were put into warm water, and revived, and were kept in Kate's room for a little while, and then were taken away and dried, and put in Martha's Bible as precious relics.

And Mrs. Estridge's letter did yet more for the country girl. There was something in its tone which roused her self-respect. Unconsciously, there came to her a touch of womanly dignity, so that Kate and her mother said she had grown ever so much older in her ways, and Mrs. Banks now and then asked herself what it was about the girl that was different from others. Mrs. Estridge's words, telling her that she was missed at Winthrop, had a great deal to say to it; but a sense of communion and kinship with a higher Friend, far more than anything else, seemed to keep Martha in a pavilion from the strife of tongues, and to lift her heart now and then into a sense of unspeakable quietness and peace.

And so, as we have said, winter was giving place to spring, and violets, and sickly-looking primroses, with blacks from London chimneys falling thickly upon them, instead of the dews of the country, were being sold in the streets; and Martha was beginning to find that the stairs were steep and the coals heavy, and the water-cans heavier still.

One very pleasant thing had come to pass; she had found courage, much to her own astonishment, to ask the district lady to walk up and pay Kate Elmhurst a visit, and the latter had discovered that Miss Armitage had been in Somersetshire, and knew Ockley Coombe, and had loved her directly. And her visitor had spoken to her words such as Kate most specially needed concerning the high dignity of suffering and of patient endurance and of cross-bearing, when the love of Jesus is in our hearts, and had reminded her that we are not to cast the cross and carry the care, but to bear the cross and cast the care on Him who careth for us. And then Kate told her about Martha; and, little by little, a firm league and covenant was established between the top attics and Miss Armitage, who used to find opportunities of saying a kind word or two to the young servant as she passed her at her work, and who one day brought the good news that she had found a better place for Mrs. Elmhurst, with employers who would, when possible, allow her to bring her work home. After this, for two days in every week, Kate had her mother with her.

It was a Sunday evening, soon after Easter, and Martha had somewhat wearily found her way to church. She could not think why she felt so tired, or why everything in the service seemed to be going on outside her like a dream; and then, when the sermon began, she found that her eyes were growing very heavy, and gradually everything faded away into a confused vision of Winthrop, and Mill Street, and Mrs. Banks; while the organ in the church sounded like a storm threatening to burst over her head.

When Mrs. Crummie, the pew-opener, made her rounds, after service was over, to put out lights, to shut pew-doors, and to take into custody stray pocket-handkerchiefs and smelling-bottles which might have been left behind, she was surprised to find Martha, whom she had noticed as a reverent, quiet attendant at church, fast asleep in the corner of one of the free seats.

In Mrs. Crummie's composition two sometimes conflicting natures were strongly developed: as a woman, she looked compassionately on the weary face; as a pew-opener, she felt it her duty to regard the matter of going to sleep in church from an official point of view.

"Young woman," she said, in a serious tone — "young woman, you'd better wake up." Then, when Martha hastily started, being touched by Mrs. Crummie on the shoulder, she was unable to resist a kindly impulse to add, "You're very tired, my dear; you'd best go home and get to sleep."

"I suppose I am," returned Martha, rousing up, and then, realizing where she was, adding humbly, "I beg your pardon, ma'am; I can't think what came over me to make me so tired. I don't think I ever went to sleep in church before."

"It's a bad habit," said Mrs. Crummie, speaking then as a pew-opener; "I always say Eutychus is an example to such as does. Think if you was in a front gallery, or even in the body, instead of free seats, how bad it would look! Indeed, I don't like to see it anywhere along my aisle, and there isn't need with such a minister as ours. This looks as if it belonged to one of the pews in the body," she continued, darting at a pocket-handkerchief which had been dropped by some passer-by; "hem-stitched and scented, and 'Rosalie' worked in flowers round the name; that's no free-seat handkerchief, and it'll have to be claimed next Sunday."

By which time Mrs. Crummie and Martha were out in the porch, and the good lady was no longer a pew-opener, but a kind motherly little woman who told Martha she looked so tired that she'd like to take her home and give her a cup of tea if her house were not too far off; failing which, she announced her determination to walk with her as far as Mill Street, "for you look most worn out, my dear; that's what you do."

"I feel queer all over to-night," said Martha; "I can't make it out; my knees seem to give in, and things seem going round in my head —"

"It's a chill, my dear," said Mrs. Crummie, confidently; "chamomile tea, warm, or a little gruel, and a hot bath going to bed, 'll set you up if anything will."

"I don't know," answered Martha; "I'm not sure whether lying quiet isn't what I seem to want most, if missus will let me go to bed."

"You're tired out — that's what you are," repeated good Mrs. Crummie, looking her companion full in the face as they passed a lamp-post; "I believe that quiet and a glass of wine, now, elder wine, warmed, with a little spice in it, would be as good as the chamomile tea for you."

Martha inwardly thought it might be much better, and went on to imagine what Mrs. Banks' reception of a request for elder wine, with a little spice in it, might be, should the idea be brought before her; and then, as she came to the door, she thanked her new friend for the kindness, and with what strength she had got up the steps into the house.

"Poor thing!" said Mrs. Crummie to herself, "she's getting done up like most of them. If only mothers knew what girls have to meet of overwork in them lodging-houses, they wouldn't send them off all alone and unbefriended like. I know I wouldn't if I had a girl of my own."

Whereupon Mrs. Crummie went home, and had a little Sunday supper over the fire which had been expected to keep itself in her absence, and which had answered to the expectation, and found out the clergyman's text in the large Bible by the help of her spectacles; having done which, she went to bed.

Martha meantime asked herself whether the world and the people in it were always divided into three divisions, first class, second class, and third class; parlors, up-stairs, and attics; body, gallery, and free-seats — Miss Graham and Rosalie in the first, and maids-of-all-work in the last; and then she felt a difficulty in getting to her room, and had to call Mrs. Elmhurst to her aid, and had a strange weary night of tossing and sleeplessness, and in the morning was obliged to own that she could not get up, and lay still, wondering whether she was very ill, and what could be the matter, and in a confused way hoping that some one would get the lodgers their breakfasts, and that Mrs. Banks would not turn her out of doors because she could not work.

Mrs. Banks was, however, very angry. She had no notion of any people under front parlors giving themselves airs and taking to their beds, and declared that Martha should go at once to the Hospital, for which she would get a ticket that morning through the district lady. "For," she added, "district ladies is good for some things, which one never sees one coming along without a look in her face and outward garments telling of an insight into coals and blankets such as is right for the poor, not to mention letters for hospitals if such can be got for those as should be sent there."

But it so happened — how Martha could hardly make out — that Miss Armitage's visit did not result in sending her to the hospital, and that Mrs. Banks remembered how a niece of hers " by the name of Sarah Ann was looking out to better herself, and might come in for a week or so to take the other girl's place if she chose to make haste and get about again;" and that Mrs. Elmhurst's work was brought home oftener than twice a week, so that she was able to care for Martha more kindly than she had ever been cared for before.

Her mistress only once came upstairs to reproach her for " taking on," and to " wonder what girls was made of that they must turn fine ladies after a week's bustling about:" at the conclusion of which strain of exhortation, even Mrs. Banks was impelled by the sight of the pale, weary face beneath her to wind up in somewhat gentler fashion, "which nevertheless if you'll be a good girl and pluck up pretty soon, I'll keep the place open for you without making any change. Sarah Ann, now, she's as strong as a church-pillar, but she's as hard to move, and as hardened to waste and riot. Though she's my own flesh and blood," continued her relative, with quite a virtuous tone of condemnation in her voice, "I couldn't say nothing else of her. It was only yesterday evening I found her eating hot toast and butter; which I toast-and-buttered her pretty well, I can tell you."

And this confidence to Martha concerning Sarah Ann's taste for toast and butter — although the illustration hurriedly selected of the church-pillar was difficult to carry out in all its bearings — seemed to form quite a link in Mrs. Banks' estimation between herself and her young servant; and she left the latter greatly cheered, and with a hope that her mistress would for this once pass over her "taking on and being ill."

Then followed a very peaceful fortnight in the region of the top-attics. Martha was astonished to find that she had so many friends in London. For kind little Mrs. Purkiss came to see her, having heard of her being ill through Mrs. Elmhurst, who had one day left word of the same at the general decorator's; and she brought with her a nice cup of jelly, and some eggs laid by her own fowls, and a general atmosphere of cheeriness and hopefulness which seemed to fill the room like a fresh breeze. And then Eliza, her own sister, came to visit her; and Mrs. Banks was quite surprised to find that Martha's sister was so capable a young servant, "holding a position," as she expressed it afterwards to Mrs. Smythe, "in a first-rate family;" and Eliza was for writing home to Winthrop; but Martha did not wish to "put them about just for her."

And after a few days, she was able to go into Kate's room, and to lie on the bed there, and read with her, and talk with her, and now and then to sleep quite undisturbedly for hours, while rest did its work towards restoring her strength. And the spring breezes came in at the window, bringing messages, Kate said, from Somersetshire, and Martha said, from Norfolk; and young sparrows twittered on the roofs; and often Miss Armitage came to them, and sometimes sang to the two girls, while their voices joined in with hers, so that, as she observed, "they made quite a choir;" and the chimes now and then sounded through the upper chamber, so that when Martha was able once more to go to her work, and to return to the hurry and bustle downstairs, it seemed to her as if a quiet restful time of peace were over to which she would look back always as to a Sunday in her life.

## CHAPTER VII.

### MARTHA HAS VISITORS.

IT happened shortly after that Mrs. Banks was laid up; and very much was she surprised at herself for being thus subjected to the vicissitudes of life like any one else. And one morning Martha came into Mrs. Elmhurst, imploring her to see about the front parlor's breakfast, as her mistress said she was "all of one throb," and couldn't fancy anything but a cup of tea, which she must bring up to her at once. After which, she was sent forth to secure once more the services of Sarah Ann, who, it appeared, had not yet succeeded in bettering herself, and who was invited to come and help in the house, there being, however, a distinct clause in the agreement whereby she was to hold herself bound honorably to abstain from any recurring temptations to indulgence in buttered toast.

It was wonderful, everybody said, how well the house went on. New responsibilities seemed to develop in Martha qualities of self-reliance and quiet womanly capability which, at first sight, her friends would hardly have suspected her of possessing; and people reflected that her mistress gave herself much unnecessary expense in the matter of words, as things settled themselves in quite a satisfactory manner without there seeming to be any necessity for so much scolding about them.

I think that a perpetual liability to being scolded and found fault with has one of two effects. Either it hardens the temper into a sort of dull or impatient sullenness; or it renders it, from the very fact of constant suffering, tender and considerate in all dealings with others, which may possibly be the result of experimentally knowing the value of a kind and sympathizing word. The last of these two effects showed itself in Martha's conduct towards her small world without; so that Kate, upstairs, and Sarah Jane, down-stairs, thought a great deal more of our Norfolk maiden's presence than she at all suspected.

And in one of these days, a sudden and unwonted knock brought her hastily to the house-door, and with an almost cry of surprise, she found herself face to face with Mr. and Mrs. Estridge, who, standing on the door-step, and wearing respectively hat and coat, and bonnet and shawl, were, she immediately concluded, not a vision, but actual Winthrop realities.

What a comfort that Mrs. and Miss Smythe were out for the day, and that Martha could fearlessly show her visitors into their parlor! What a comfort that Sarah Ann was well-disposed towards her, and, having listened at the bottom of the stairs to the strange greetings, was prepared to answer Martha's hurried whisper down the same flight, " You'll turn the joint, won't you?" with a comprehensive "All right, I'll see to everything!"

And then the Winthrop girl went in to the front parlor, and realized that to see her, Martha Brooke, these friends had come miles across London — that nothing else had brought them down into Southwark but the desire to visit and cheer the young maid-of-all-work, "whom they had not forgotten," as she said to herself, " in all their greatness."

O if only she were less tongue-tied! O if only she could tell Mrs. Estridge how she thanked her, and loved her. and cared for her! As it was, she could only muster courage to ask for her parents, and to utter confused words of humble gratitude, and then, all of a sudden — she supposed because she had been ill and was still weak and foolish — she found, as she thanked Mrs. Estridge for the photograph she had brought her of Winthrop church. that her voice was getting beyond control. and that tears were coming thickly into her eyes, and a hurried sob or two for a minute entirely checked every possibility of utterance.

Then her friends talked to her, and Mrs. Estridge told her Winthrop news of her class companions, and of her brothers and sisters; and after awhile, she found herself able to speak more freely; and when they thought that she looked thin and worn, she told them how she had been ill, and about Miss Armitage and Kate and Mrs. Elmhurst; and at last, actually found herself saying how she had missed her Winthrop Sundays, and longed to be once more at the Rectory class.

"But you keep up?" answered Mrs. Estridge, with her hand upon her shoulder in the same kindly fashion which she remembered so well and had thought of so often, "You are trying to serve Jesus Christ, dear child, and to be His faithful soldier and servant in all the busy hurry and work of your life? I hope you are looking to Him, Martha."

And then with a sort of smile through her tears, Martha looked up, and said, "I'm trying to keep the Christmas chimes going in my heart, like the message said that you gave us, ma'am; sometimes when I'm dull and tired I feel as if I must give in; but then I say to myself I'm to keep it always going—'Thanks be to God for His Unspeakable Gift'—and that seems to set me up."

The visit did not end in the front parlor. Martha brought them to see Kate, and Kate's eyes lighted up when she knew who the visitors were, and while Mr. Estridge talked to the girls about the struggle and the weariness and the difficulties here which are but for a little while, and about the great joy laid up which is reserved unto the Lord's people for ever. And then he knelt down, and thanked God for the Unspeakable Gift, and asked that they might always be living as those who have tasted of eternal life through Jesus Christ our Lord, and prayed for the sick, and the weary, and the hard-working, that they might come unto Him and find rest for their souls. And then that golden hour in Martha's life came to an end, and her friends left her; and she watched them, until, turning round the corner of Mill Street, they nodded a last good-bye to her, and went their way.

And Martha went back to her work; and found that Sarah Ann had been true to her and to the joint, and that it was time to lay the cloth in the front parlor.

As Mr. and Mrs. Estridge walked away they were for a few minutes very silent. Then Mr. Estridge looked into his wife's face, and saw that her eyes were full of tears.

"Good little Martha!" he said; "how little one could expect to find such a girl out of the Brookes' cottage."

"Charles," answered his wife, after a pause, "I feel as if Martha had taught me more than I ever taught her. I shall never hear our Winthrop bells now without thinking of her, in all the hurry and care of that rough life of hers trying to keep the Christmas chimes ringing. It will help me to do it when I think of her. If only — if only one could think every day more of the greatness of the Unspeakable Gift!"

## CHAPTER VIII.

### LAST WORDS.

 KNOW that my story may be called unfinished. It is so because it is true. In a busy and thronged London district, and in a busy and thronged house, a little maid-of-all-work is still trying to keep the chime going in her heart — is still trying to show forth praise not only with her lips, but in her life.

And would not this busy and thronged world, this great lodging-house in which for a time we have our habitation, be to many who read these pages a happier and a better place could they have constantly in their minds the greatness of the "Unspeakable Gift," the belief in a real present, living, loving Saviour;

could they, too, keep the chimes of joy and thanksgiving always ringing?

*Busy workers*, in whatever station of life you may be placed, who have found time to read these words, shall not they sound in your hearts? There is room in them for the clang and uproar of the world's noise and tumult: is there not room for the sweet cadence of peace and thanksgiving which follows the admission of Jesus, and which rings in the true Christmas-tide of the soul? It may be that you are at the head of a family, and have calls and claims and interruptions on every side, and "many coming and going," so that sometimes you seem to have "no leisure to tarry so much as to eat." Or it may be that you are a servant, always busy, often tired, sometimes overtasked; or possibly you are a boy or girl at school, and have your time portioned out for you, and find that every moment is fully occupied. Still, let the chime ring in your hearts. Ask the Lord Jesus Christ to come to you Himself. Make time for Him, for whatever else you may find no leisure. "What shall it profit a man if he shall gain the whole world and lose his own soul?" He wants to be the Friend of your busy hours. He wants to make your work light by making your heart light. He wants to make your common every-day service holy and beautiful and happy service, by letting you do all as for Him. He wants to share, and help you, in all your work, and to prove to you that He is a true and present Saviour.

It may be that you are specially engaged in sacred work; that you are a teacher, a district visitor, a much-employed vineyard laborer. O, should not those thus occupied be very earnest in making sure that the chime is ringing in their hearts? Is not something of the peace which should come with the constantly realized possession of the Unspeakable Gift endangered by the too great hurry of our days — by the effort to crowd too much into already fully employed hours — by the mistaken idea that to do much *for* Christ is the same thing as keeping near *to* Christ? It is when we have time to be still, when the world is shut out, when our work is brought to Him in prayer, when the unseen things of eternity are the vividly seen things of our souls, when " there is no man found with us save Jesus only," that the clear notes of thanksgiving swell most joyfully through our hearts, and

"Sound like the benediction
Which follows after prayer."

Perhaps you may be reading this *on a sick-bed*. It may be that you are an invalid, confined to a couch from which you will never again rise to health and strength, or suffering in a hospital, or weak and failing, and unable for all the work without, which you are longing to undertake, and which may even be left undone because you cannot do it. I think that for you it is hardest of all to keep the chimes going. I think that to you, if you seek to turn mourning into thankfulness, the message will be most specially sent, " He that offereth me praise, he honoreth me." I hardly know any victory of faith so great as that won by Christ's servants when they are able to rejoice in tribulation; in weakness to obtain strength; in weariness to lean on an unseen Saviour; during sleepless nights to look beyond to the everlasting rest; when all around them are busy and in health, to whisper, "Even so, Father;" to pray, saying, "Thy will be done," and to exchange the sad minor strain, "*My* purposes are broken off," for the trustful song of assurance:

> "*His* purposes will ripen fast,
> Unfolding every hour:
> The bud may have a bitter taste,
> But sweet will be the flower."

It is no light service which you are offering to Jesus, dear brother or sister, in your hour of weakness, if you are able to cry, "Though He slay me, yet will I trust in Him," if you are rejoicing in the Unspeakable Gift, and keeping the chime of thanksgiving always ringing in your heart.

Perhaps you are *poor*. Possibly you find it hard to keep down anxious fears concerning a coming year, or an impending difficulty, or to check forebodings which will arise in your heart when but little comes in, and there seem to crowd upon you increasing claims for what you have. Then, if you have the Unspeakable Gift, you may take the children's privilege, and expect your Father to care for you. A good man once said, "On the forehead of every one of God's people are inscribed the words, *To be provided for.*" Only trust. "He that spared not His own Son, but delivered Him up for us all, how shall He not with Him freely also give us all things?" If you have Christ, though having nothing, you possess all things. God cannot desert you; His gift of a Saviour is the pledge that He will give you all that you really need. Try and cling to Him. He will help you, even in your poverty, to set the joy-bells ringing in your heart, and to offer "thanks unto Him for His Unspeakable Gift."

It may be that you are *lonely* — that you are away from those dearest to you — that you are surrounded by many who cannot sympathize with you — that harsh and irritating words bring continual uneasiness and pain to your heart, and that you have no one upon whom you can lean for companionship and support. Then seek these in Jesus. I do not say that it is easy to realize the nearness, the love, the confidence of an unseen Saviour. I do not think it is. But I know that these may be, and are, felt by His children who, not having seen, yet have believed. If in the hour of loneliness you are brought near to Him — if you are enabled to realize the truth of His Word, "Draw nigh to God, and He will draw nigh to you,"— you will arise to find great peace within your heart, the song coming from your lips, "It is good for me to draw nigh unto God," and the chime already sounding in unspoken praise.

One word more to any reader of these pages who may be amongst the *bereaved*. Can there be any joyful strain for you until the chimes of heaven welcome you to reunion with those — your beloved — who have gone before? Here, where at every moment you miss the answering voice and look and companionship which will never more waken you to a constant delight, can you desire or expect anything beyond submission and the peace of resignation? Is any sound to echo through the inner temple of your heart but the secret knell heard in still watches of the night, in the early wakings of the morning, and in the midst of others' joys which seem to ripple round in waves of gladness, but between which and your secret soul there is a line of separation which you feel can never be passed?

I think that He who is the Resurrection and the Life may even to you bring such a sense of the greatness of the Unspeakable Gift, that, "Thanks be unto God," will ring through your heart with a joy different from all others — that which comes from being a partaker with Christ of sorrow, and a partaker of His consolations — that which comes from the intimacy with Him into which grief and bereavement admit His children — that of which He Himself spake, saying, "Your joy no man taketh from you."

Yes, we must "keep the chimes going" here, in the time of our warfare and pilgrimage; "church bells," as old George Herbert hath it, "above the starres hearde."

And He who hears them above the stars is the Same who hath said, "In my Father's house are many mansions: I go to prepare a place for you. And if I go and prepare a place for you, I will come again and receive you unto Myself, that where I am there ye may be also."

Cambridge: Press of John Wilson and Son.

# A LIST OF BOOKS

## PUBLISHED BY

# E. P. DUTTON AND CO.,

### 135 Washington Street, Boston.

|  | PRICE |
|---|---|
| Ancient Psalm Melodies | $0.35 |
| Anyta, and other Poems, by George H. Calvert | 1.25 |
| Approbation Cards, per hundred | 1.00 |
| Baptism Certificates, on cards | 6 |
| Bertha Weisser's Wish | 75 |
| Bickersteith's Devout Communicant | 50 |
| Blackboard Brushes | .38 and .50 |
| Bolles on Confirmation | 10 |
| Boy Artists | 1.00 |
| Burgess's Questions on the Ecclesiastical Year | 15 |
| Burgess's (Bishop) Last Journal, paper, 50 cts.; cloth | 75 |
| Cammann's Exposition of Church Catechism | 15 |
| Canticles of the Church, paper, 25 cts.; cloth | 50 |
| Canticles, Hymns, and Carols | 25 |
| Carols for Christmas, &c., by A. P. Howard | 60 |
| Catechism of the Church | 2 |
| Chapman's Sermons on the Church | 1.75 |
| Cheerily, Cheerily, etc., A Christmas Carol | 6 |
| Children's Songs from the Hill-sides | 2.00 |
| Choice Consolation | 1.25 |
| Christian Education, a tract by the Rev. Morgan Dix, S. T. D. | 6 |
| Christian Witness and Church Advocate, per year | 4.00 |
| Christmas Holidays at Cedar Grove | 1.00 |
| Collects, paper, 15 cents; cloth | 30 |
| Confirmation Certificates, on card | 6 |

|  | PRICE |
|---|---|
| Contraband Christmas............................ | $0.75 |
| Cushions and Corners............................ | 1.00 |
| | |
| Daily Hymns; or, Hymns for Every Day in Lent.... | 1.00 |
| Dark Mountains.................................. | 60 |
| Dark River...................................... | 60 |
| Digest of Canons, paper, 75 cents; cloth............ | 1.25 |
| Divine Life and the New Birth..................... | 1.50 |
| Doctrine of the Trinity........................... | 10 |
| | |
| Easter Holidays at Cedar Grove.................... | 75 |
| Elim; or, Hymns of Holy Refreshment............. | 2.00 |
| | |
| Faithful Promiser................................ | 25 |
| Fanny and Robbie................................ | 75 |
| First Bereavement................................ | 25 |
| Follow Thou Me................................. | 20 |
| Fowle's Common School Grammar................. | 35 |
| Fowle's Physiological Diagrams.................... | 8.00 |
| Fowle's Physiology............................... | 50 |
| Frank Stirling's Choice........................... | 1.00 |
| Free Evening Service............................. | 25 |
| | |
| Gentleman, The, by George H. Calvert............. | 1.25 |
| Globes.................................. 5.00 to | 62.50 |
| Golden Censer................................... | 1.25 |
| Good News of God............................... | 1.75 |
| Griswold's Prayers............................... | 1.25 |
| | |
| Haskins's What is Confirmation?.................. | 12 |
| Historical Church................................ | 10 |
| Holiday Library, 6 vols........................... | 4.50 |
| Hours with the Lord............................. | 30 |
| Howard's Collection of Carols............... 60 and | 1.00 |
| Huntington's (Rev. F. D.) Tracts, each............ | 10 |
| Huntington's (Rev. F. D.) Sermons for the People.. | 1.75 |
| Huntington's (Rev. F. D.) Christian Believing, etc. | 1.75 |
| Huntington's (Rev. F. D.) Lessons on the Parables. | 30 |
| Huntington's (Rev. Wm. R.) Questions............ | 30 |
| Hymns by Harriet McEwen Kimball. ............. | 1.50 |

|  | PRICE. |
|---|---|
| Ides's School Registers | $0.25 to 2.00 |
| Imitation of Christ | 1.50 and 2.00 |
| Intercessory Prayer | 50 |
| | |
| Jesus Lives: An Easter Carol | 6 |
| Journey Home | 60 |
| | |
| Keble's Christian Year | 1.50 and 2.00 |
| Kimball's (Miss) Hymns | 1.50 |
| | |
| Laud (Abp.), Life of | 1.25 |
| Lee's Family Prayers | 1.25 |
| Leon and Zephie | 75 |
| Lessons on the Liturgy | 1.25 |
| Little Folks, by Oscar Pletsch | 1.25 |
| Lowell's (Rev. Robert) Poems | 1.25 |
| Lyra Domestica | 1.50 |
| Lyra Germanica | 1.25 |
| | |
| Mann's Lectures on Education | 1.25 |
| Maps, &c. | |
| Marriage Certificates | 6 |
| Mason's Sermons | 4.00 |
| Mind of Jesus | 35 |
| Mind, and Promiser | 50 |
| Miss Matty | 75 |
| Monro's Allegories, each | 60 |
| Monthly Report Cards, per hundred | 1.00 |
| | |
| Ned Grant's Quest | 1.00 |
| New Priest in Conception Bay | 1.75 |
| Numerical Frames | 1.25 and 1.50 |
| | |
| Old Corner Library, 4 vols. | 4.00 |
| Old, Old Story | 15 |
| Ottalie's Stories | 1.50 |
| Oxenden's Our Church and Her Services | 60 and 1.00 |
| | |
| Parting Spirit's Address | 25 and 1.00 |

|  | PRICE |
|---|---|
| Party Spirit in the Church | $0.50 and 0.75 |
| Pietas Quotidiana | 60 |
| Prayer-Books | 0.50 to 20.00 |
| Prayer-Book, Rubricated | 6.00 to 20.00 |
| Proper Lessons | 1.25 to 4.00 |
| Psalms and Hymns of the Prayer-Book | 60 |
| | |
| Queen : A Story for Girls | 75 |
| | |
| Rector's Vade Mecum | 1.00 to 3.00 |
| Restoration of Belief, by Isaac Taylor | 1.50 |
| Robinson's Book-Keeping and Blanks, each | 25 |
| Rock of Ages | 1.25 |
| | |
| Sacred Gems for Letters, two pages | 1 |
| Sewell's Preparation for Holy Communion | 75 |
| Sewell's Thoughts for Holy Week | 50 |
| Silence of Scripture | 1.00 |
| Shnik Shnak, by Oscar Pletsch | 1.25 |
| Story of the New Priest | 1.75 |
| Sunday-School Chant and Tune-Book | 50 |
| Sunday-School Prayer-Book | 40 |
| Sunday-School Prayer-Book and Chant and Tune-Book, half-bound, 60 cents; bev. cloth | 1 00 |
| | |
| Teacher's Coöperating Mirrors, per hundred | 1.50 |
| Teacher's Weekly Report Cards, per hundred | 1.50 |
| Trinity Psalter | 1.75 |
| | |
| Vinton's (Rev. Alex. H.) Sermons | 1.50 |
| | |
| Wainwright's Family Prayers | 1.25 |
| Wainwright's Short Family Prayers | 50 |
| Waiting World | 20 |
| Waring's Hymns and Meditations | 1.25 |
| Winter and Summer at Burton Hall | 1.00 |
| Words of Jesus | 35 |
| Words, and Promiser | 50 |
| Words, Mind, and Promiser | 1.00 |

# Children's Books.

Making this a special department in our business, we have been careful in the selection of our publications; it being our aim to issue books healthy and moral in their tone, and at the same time fresh and entertaining to children. We invite purchasers to examine the following, feeling convinced they will find them much beyond the average of Children's Books. They are all printed in clear type, on good paper, beautifully illustrated, and bound in bright colors.

### NEW BOOKS.

**LITTLE FOLKS.** 20 Illustrations by Oscar Pletsch, with verses of appropriate poetry accompanying each picture, beautifully printed. Large 8vo. $1.25.

**SHNIK SHNAK.** 20 Illustrations by Oscar Pletsch. A companion volume to the above. $1.25.

"Oscar Pletsch is remarkable for his genius in sketching children. Not Hogarth or Gustave Doré was ever more eminent in their line than Pletsch is in his." — *Publishers' Circular.*

"His pictures are not only drawn with masterly accuracy and skill, but they are wonderfully true to nature, and show a rare faculty of embodying the humorous element in the occupations and expressions of childhood." — *The Nursery.*

"What Landseer is to dogs, what Rosa Bonheur is to horses, what Morland is to pigs, what Teniers is to Dutch boors, Oscar Pletsch is to children, — their painter, interpreter, immortalizer." — *Boston Transcript.*

"In the humor and fidelity of his pictures of children, Pletsch is without a rival in the whole range of art."

**BOY ARTISTS;** or, Sketches of the Childhood of Michael Angelo, Mozart, Haydn, Watteau, and Sebastian Gomez. Translated from the French of Mdlle. Eugenie Foa. 16mo. Illustrated.......$1.00

Our critic says: "The French biographical stories of Madame

Foa, are very life-like, interesting, and well worth reproduction in English dress. I would certainly recommend their publication, for they are very attractive."

**COPSLEY ANNALS**, Preserved in Proverbs. 16mo. bevelled boards, red edge. $1.25.

" The family histories here described are commendable in no common degree; full of a sweet and gentle spirit, without sickliness; religious in tone and the high morals inculcated, without a trace of such sectarianism as would exclude them from the fireside of church or chapel-goer; not without nice touches of humor, clear of exaggeration. It must be a healthy pleasure to write — it is to read — such books for the young as 'Copsley Annals.' " — *Athenæum*.

"A delightful book, and one which will afford pleasant entertainment to readers, old and young. A thoroughly good and well-written story." — *Record*.

"Here is wit, tenderness, and good writing enough for twice as large a volume. It is altogether a most fascinating performance, likely to please poor and rich, young and old."— *Literary Churchman*.

**WINTER AND SUMMER AT BURTON HALL.** By the author of " Cushions and Corners." 16mo. Illustrated......................$1.00

We take pleasure in offering to the thousands who have read " Cushions and Corners" with delight, another book by the same charming writer. Before deciding to reprint it, we gave the English copy to several children to read, and our juvenile jury returned the unanimous verdict that it was one of the best stories they had ever read.

**CUSHIONS AND CORNERS** : or, Holidays at Old Orchard. New Edition. 16mo. Illustrated. 214 pages. Price reduced to $1.00.

"A capital delineation of childish character, the conversations are managed very naturally, and the contrast between the dispositions, so well symbolized by a cushion and a sharp corner, respectively, is wrought out skilfully, and in a most interesting manner." — *The Nation*.

"The author has humor and dramatic power, and an appreciation of children's tastes ; the book has a good moral besides." — *Springfield Republican.*

### NED GRANT'S QUEST. A Story for Children.
By the author of "Bertha Weisser's Wish." 195 pages. Price reduced to $1.00.

" The young folks who are so fortunate as to get hold of this book will follow the fortunes of Ned Grant with great interest." — *Providence Press.*

" The writer is one of our best story-tellers, and this is such a book as goes right to the heart of a boy." — *Churchman.*

### FRANK STIRLING'S CHOICE. By Maria H. Bulfinch. Price reduced to $1.00.

" Christian parents may do much good by placing this book in the hands of every bright and thoughtful boy."

" An excellent story of a boyhood and youth ending in the ministry of the Church." — *Advertiser.*

### FANNIE AND ROBBIE. A Year Book for Children of the Church. Price 75 cents.

" Fannie wished to do some good in Lent, and sought out Robbie, the lame son of a poor widow, as a subject. She read to him, taught him about the Christian Seasons; when he got well took him to the Sunday-school, and so became useful." — *Connecticut Churchman.*

" The interest is well sustained, and youth of both sexes will read it with pleasure." — *Protestant Churchman.*

### MISS MATTY ; or, Our Youngest Passenger. A Tale of the Sea. Price 75 cents.

" A capital sea-story, with natural scenes and characters, and incidents that thrill with interest." — *Albany Argus.*

" Another book that we can highly praise. Any small man or woman, who, after reading it, would not be better, or would not try to be better — for the spirit may be willing, the flesh weak — ought hardly to be taught to read at all, or made to learn twice over." — *The Nation.*

"**THE OLD CORNER LIBRARY.**" Containing: — Ned Grant's Quest, Frank Stirling's Choice, Cushions and Corners, and Christmas Holidays at Cedar Grove.  4 vols. in box.  Price $4.00.

"Four juvenile publications, handsome in form, tasteful in illustrations, interesting in matter, and pure in moral tone." — *Transcript.*

**THE HOLIDAY LIBRARY.**  Containing: — Miss Matty, Fannie and Robbie, Easter Holidays at Cedar Grove, Bertha Weisser, Contraband Christmas, and A Queen.  6 vols. in box.  Price $4.50.

"All good stories, as the little ones tell us." — *Boston Post*

**CHILDREN'S SONGS FROM THE HILLSIDE.**  A beautifully illustrated volume of Poetry for Children.  Bevelled boards, gilt edge, $2.00.

"This book of songs will be warmly welcomed by a multitude of households all over the land.  These verses were written for children, but both old age and youth will read them with delight." — *Christian Times.*

"A charming collection of songs, poems, and charades for the little ones.  Illustrated by Kilburn in admirable taste, printed on satin paper at the 'Riverside Press,' and bound in bright colors and gold, it is, every way, a perfect thing."

**OTTALIE'S STORIES FOR THE LITTLE FOLKS.**  Translated from the German of Madame Ottalie Wildermuth; containing the following stories, bound together: —

>   Frau Luna, and Her Voyages.
>   A Queen, A Story for Girls.
>   Leon and Zephie; or, the Little Wanderers.

16mo, 308 pages, 4 fine wood-cuts······$1.50.

www.ingramcontent.com/pod-product-compliance
Lightning Source LLC
Chambersburg PA
CBHW030302170426
43202CB00009B/848